WHOLEHEARTED

THE CROSSING

Jeff Ecklund

Copyright © 2017—Jeff Ecklund

All rights reserved. This book is protected by the copyright laws of the United States of America. This book may not be copied or reprinted for commercial gain or profit. The use of short quotations or occasional page copying for personal or group study is encouraged. Permission will be granted upon request from Jeff Ecklund. Unless otherwise stated, all biblical quotations are taken from the New American Standard Version. All rights reserved. Any emphasis added to Scripture quotations is the author's own.

First Printing: 2017

ISBN-13: 978-1544008578

Cover design by Amani Hanson (Becoming Studios, noboxez@yahoo.com).

Editing, text design and typesetting by Jim Bryson (JamesLBryson@gmail.com).

Proofreading by Em Zorne (pcome.proofandcopy@gmail.com)

Endorsements

Everyone has a mountain within that they should fight to win! Successful Christian living seems like an uphill battle to overcome both imperfect character and real life enemies at times, but in the secret place God inspires the courage needed for redemptive spiritual victory. This brilliant overview of Caleb and Joshua's quest to serve God is woven together with personal stories, as well as practical, modern, everyday-life issues. It encourages the wilderness traveler, the skeptical doubter, the weary fighter, the lost wanderer and even those who already have hope and faith that God is willing to equip them all with miraculous strength, skill, wisdom and every piece of armor that is necessary to win the promises and rewards that He has for them.

Dr. Stan Fleming

Gate Breaker Ministries

*****

My good friend, Jeff Ecklund, has provided a pathway to your purpose and destiny. The Psalmist David tells us in Psalms 23, that our Good Shepherd will, "lead us in paths of righteousness for His Name's sake." This great book on the journey of Joshua and Caleb provides a clear roadmap. Bathed in Scripture and life experience, *Wholehearted-The Crossing*, is what it looks like when

Biblical truth is incarnated into the life of a Jesus-follower like Jeff. This book will speak to men and women. This book will speak to pastors and lay-people. This book will speak to everybody. Jeff's writing style is conversational yet poignant. Some of the stories are hilarious, yet packed with life-proven truths that will challenge and encourage anyone looking for solid guidance on the journey of life.

   Doug Sherman
   Lead Pastor
   Grace Harvest Church

*****

One of my life scriptures comes from Deuteronomy 31:6 when Moses said to Joshua, "Be strong and of good courage, do not fear nor be afraid of them; for the Lord your God, He is the One who goes with you. He will not leave you nor forsake you." Jeff unpacks many truths with scriptures and great illustrations that will help you be strong and courageous in your wholehearted pursuit of God. This is a great book for personal study as well as group discussion.

   Dick Iverson
   Founder
   City Bible Church
   Portland Bible College
   Ministers Fellowship International

*****

In reading *Wholehearted-The Crossing*, I have once again been fired up and made aware that I was made for greatness. All of us were. I will not settle! I will not drift!

I'm afraid that after forty years of ministry, my sight of the promises may have become a bit obscured. And yet, I have prided myself as one who is determined to always be firing on all cylinders. As for me, this book served as a first class "spiritual tune-up." Once again I have my eyes on a few more mountains that are rightfully mine and that I intend take!

A life spent serving God is not a snapshot, it's a video. In Pastor Jeff's book *Wholehearted-The Crossing*, the reader is privileged to fast forward to the end of Caleb's life. It is there that the life of this great man shows us that no one or no-thing can stop a wholehearted warrior of God. For those who live your lives wholeheartedly, your rewards are ahead, your inheritance is sure, and God's promises are yea and amen! The life of Caleb as well as that of the author, whom I have observed for twenty-five years, leaves us begging the question, "Why would anyone choose to live a life with less than a whole heart?"

In the life of Caleb, as well as that of our author's, I have observed once again that in the Kingdom of God the way up is down! In the end, it is the heart of a man that propels him upward.

I have many wonderful friends serving in ministry. Pastor Jeff and his dear wife Robie are among them. While there are some whom I wish I could know what they know, there are others whom I wish I could be what they are! Pastor Jeff and Robie are among those of the latter

Pastor Don Metcalf
Desert Reign
Cerritos Ca

*****

This book is a winner!

With so many books available today, I have to be choosy. *Wholehearted-The Crossing* was worthy of my time. In each of the thirty-one short chapters, Jeff masterfully paints relevant thought-provoking pictures. He shows us that God not only wants us to recognize & truly know that His ways, strength and thoughts are higher, but He desires to elevate us to His level of victorious, grand Joshua & Caleb-like thinking & action through Jesus.

I would like to challenge you to take this journey with Jeff and let him show how your life could take on epic proportions. To lead you out of the flat lands & toward the "mountainous" life God has purposed for you. Could you be believing a lie and settling for less? Living beneath your priveledges when God has a mountain with you & your children's name on it?

This could be your God-moment to take the Caleb dare, to move to a "life with a million dollar view," to live WHOLEHEARTED!

Ralph Lowe
Lead Pastor, Legacy Church,
Meridian, Idaho

Appreciation

My life has been shaped and influenced by relationships from early on, as well as the sharpening that happens during the journey, much of which I didn't fully appreciate until later in life. During the times that I was interacting with family, friends, mentors and even antagonists, something was being forged within me that God would use throughout my life.

My first thank you is to the great rescue of my life perpetrated by Jesus. I cannot imagine where I would be without his pursuit and my surrender.

After that, my greatest support is my wife Robie. No one has believed in me, prayed for and with me as she has. She is a fierce friend and I could not have completed this project without her support.

My sons, Drew and Joel, along with their beautiful wives Rachel and Lindsey (and the grandchildren that keep coming!)

To my extended family that is so large (I am one of ten siblings), I am grateful to be part of a root system so strong.

To the mentors, leaders and brothers in Christ who have helped the shaping of my life—I would not be the same without your influence. My spiritual father, Til Hanson, other key influencers like Don Metcalf, Joseph Thornton, Roy Roberts, Ralph Lowe, Matt Studer, Ted Hoit, Larry Terherst. Harold Eberle—you and Linda opened doors of ministry that we did not know existed. Thanks for also introducing me to my first writing coach, Jim Bryson, who has challenged me and is continuing to teach me to write.

Also to the network of leaders in Ministers Fellowship International who have resourced and encouraged our life and ministry, as well as becoming friends.

Doug & Peggy Sherman, thanks for being friends and loving our family. Bob and Cindy Johnson, Bob and Cara Grimm, Jonathon and Raydean Owens, Frank and Sharon Damazio as well as Bob and Sue Macgregor. When we have any of you come in to minister at our church, I am often asked, "Where did you find these people?" My reply is always, "They are our friends"! So many others and not room to list them all.

Last but not least, the beautiful churches that have welcomed us, allowed us to lead and that ministered to us along the way. New Life Church in Okanogan, where we were trained, equipped and sent out. Mountain Life Church in McCall was our first lead destination and we certainly learned a lot and were blessed both by the beauty of the people and the surrounding area. And to the House of the Lord. When we came here ten years ago, I was approached by a lady who boldly stated, "God must really love you to bring you here to this church; she is very special." And you know? It's so true. Our amazing team of elders (Brian and Cindy, Dave and Rhoda, Cary and Lonnie, and Joel and Lindsey). And other leaders there as well as friends and congregation. You make it a joy to serve and walk together.

Thanks to all who have supported us. It is humbling and we are honored.

Jeff & Robie Ecklund

Contents

Foreword..iii

Preface..iv

Introduction..ix

See Things Differently............................1

Declarations of Faith..............................7

There is an Inheritance........................21

Live Differently......................................25

We Can Drive Out Giants....................31

The Land Can Rest From War............37

Joshua The Crossing............................43

Stop Focusing on the Past...................47

No Journey Alone.................................53

God-Ordained Things Are Ahead......59

The Tent of Meeting.............................65

Faith Crosses Rivers.............................73

Word Up!..81

Positioning to Pursue...........................89

Made To Be Different..........................93

Made for Promotion............................97

Willing Power..........................105

Available Men..........................119

Making Memories.....................125

The Why of the Wilderness.................131

The Heart in the Wilderness...............137

Wilderness Strong.....................145

Stronger Together....................155

The Marking..........................167

Overcoming Opposition.....................173

Testimony That Changes History........183

The Achan In All Of Us......................191

Back to the Tent!.............................201

Facing Your Failure..........................209

Kings of Opposition........................217

A Longing Fulfilled..........................225

About The Author..........................229

Foreword

By Dr. Harold Eberle

Crossing over begins in the heart. Whether you are a gnarly warrior of yore or a harried businessperson on Wall Street, eventually you will be presented an opportunity disguised as an obstacle. In *Wholehearted – The Crossing*, Jeff Ecklund unravels the ways in which God transitions us to higher callings and greater blessings. Using the pattern established through the lives of Caleb and Joshua of the Old Testament, we are led on a detailed study of Israel's transition from slave nation to possessors of the Promised Land. Along the way, we learn of the men who led her.

I can't imagine what it's like to physically fight for my life. Like many of Jeff's readers, my battles are spiritual and societal. Still, I've faced my share of foes. I've stood confounded at challenges I could not see beyond and honestly questioned God's wisdom for leading me into some of the difficult places I've had to fight my way through. None of this would mean anything, however, were it not for the loving hand of God demonstrating himself in power and wisdom. Everything I've ever faced and overcome required a crossing—leaving one shore, accepting a transitionary state of flux, and arriving equipped for battle on the opposite shore. I am living testimony to the saving power of God that can lead us into greater depths of His Spirit. Allow me to state categorically that the fundamental requirement for success in this life and beyond—for make no mistake about it: success is never guaranteed—is to be wholehearted.

Those who think their destiny is all sewn up by virtue of a live human birth mistake the purpose of our free will before Almighty God. Yes, He who sends us forth to fulfill our calling also prepares us for the challenges ahead. Yet every battle is a test, just as every test is an opportunity. In the end, we decide to fight or run, charge or hide, and learn to treat the twin imposters of success and failure as prerequisites for greater accomplishment. There is only one mistake we can make in battle, and that is to hold back that vital part of ourselves—our heart.

Israel made it to the Promised Land, as Jeff shows us, but not every Israelite made it to the Promised Land. Indeed, an entire generation of unbelievers had to die off before Israel's destiny could be fulfilled. So it is today. God's purposes will be accomplished. His Kingdom will cover the earth. And all creation will bow before him. The question is…will you?

So give in now. Accept that being wholehearted is the only way to walk in God. The battle will be easier, the victories swifter, and the lessons clearer. There are no half-hearted winners in war, only carnage.

Wholehearted – The Crossing is for every man who ever looked into the mirror dreading what he'd find; for every woman who has ever tried to love him; for every person striving day and night for something greater in the Kingdom of God; and for the Lord who sees, hears, and leads us through our passions and into His purposes. This book is for you.

May you find all that God has put in your heart.

Dr. Harold R. Eberle, Worldcast Ministries

Preface

Devotions To Move Us Forward

My wife tells of a night more than twenty years ago, when I sat straight up in bed from a deep sleep, raised my hand and declared: "Someday, I am going to write a book!" I then promptly dropped back to sleep. Years later, I finally have completed this project.

Now that it is complete, I often wonder what kept me so long from writing. When you are young, there is a sense of time going slowly. The diversions, distractions and good things of life keep us from achieving great things…and life just happens. I'm not sure we understand how the pace of the culture today can devour hours, days, months and ultimately years and decades, but it does.

I spent some time as a child on my grandparent's ranch in Northern Idaho and remember the "party line" phone system. If the landline phone rang twice it was yours, if it was one or three times it was someone calling one of the various neighbors sharing the same line. I hesitate to date myself, but growing up, the only remote control we had for the three television channels was one of the kids running back and forth to change the channels or reposition the rabbit ear antenna. That was a different pace compared to the speed of technology and business today. Sure, there are great advances in our culture, but diversions and distractions as well.

Although I've written songs, poems and sermon outlines for a number of years, the elusive book has been just that. Elusive! It's taken some time, but I'm convinced that inspiration without any perspiration only leads to an unnatural death of great dreams and ideas. I say "unnatural death" because when those dreams originate in the heart of God, there is a responsibility for us to partner with the Great Depositor and fulfill them!

So, with prompting and encouragement from a number of great people including mentors, peers, friends and folks I've had the privilege to teach, I've answered the call with the book you are reading. My aim is to offer the insights I've gleaned, through study and prayer, from the lives and stories of Caleb and Joshua, compiling them into a devotional that will capture the hearts of men and women.

May this work encourage, challenge, and most importantly, transform your walk with Jesus!

Introduction

> *⁶But Joshua the son of Nun and Caleb the son of Jephunneh, who were among those who had spied out the land, tore their clothes; ⁷and they spoke to all the congregation of the children of Israel, saying: "The land we passed through to spy out is an exceedingly good land. ⁸If the Lord delights in us, then He will bring us into this land and give it to us, 'a land which flows with milk and honey.'"*
>
> Numbers 14:6–8 (NKJV)

CALEB

A man with skin like worn leather walks the earth. He's hard bitten and gray with eyes keen and clear. You'd never guess his age of eighty-five as you watched his forceful gait and lean muscle barely concealed beneath his robes. There is something unmistakable about a warrior—smooth, purposeful movements; no wasted motion; scars from countless battles marking his body yet not diminishing his heart and spirit. Surely, there must have been defeats in his life, but you would not guess that by the way he carries himself. Intimidating? Yes. But the man you'd want in a fight.

This is Caleb, a man of God, the likes of which the earth needs now.

My physical description may not be accurate, but based on biblical accounts, it captures his spirit. As the Caleb and his men moved forward into the land promised to the Jews by God, I believe Caleb was amazed at the literal promise before him. Ingrained within his heart was the promise given to his forefathers Abraham, Isaac, and Jacob. Now he was walking in the fulfillment of that promise—lush farmland, abundant wildlife, a promise and hope for a better future. He'd been longing for this moment his entire life, and there it was—just on the other side of the Jordan river! What before he had only imagined, now he could see and smell. Freedom! It was no longer just hope and dreams, but a reality unfolding. The final journey had begun.

Born Under a Curse

Fear, uncertainty and pain filled the air. Jephunneh gazed upon his wife as she labored on a stool. Two women attended her on either side, supporting her arms, wiping her brow, giving her water. This was the Hebrew custom for birth. Her breath came short and painful. She longed to resume pushing, waiting for the signal from the midwife standing before her. God had somehow given them the favor of a midwife who would not obey the command of Pharaoh to kill this baby should it be a boy. At least they hoped. Some babies made it, others not. The Egyptian guard had left more than an hour ago, lured into the belief that the birth would not happen for a few more days at least. His disgust and hatred was evident as he considered the growing number of the Hebrew people in the city. The guard spat toward the house as he left, muttering under his breath something about dogs. He had to move on to another hut; there were not enough guards to monitor every situation.

Jephunneh observed his departure and gave the attendants a sign to restart the efforts. Avoiding the Egyptian guards would buy them time to guard the life of this new one. Still, a death sentence hung over the Hebrew people like a mist. Into this realm, a new son was born to Jephunneh, a boy he would name Caleb.

Color Commentary

My point in adding colorful context to the life of Caleb is simple—he did not start out well. Yet God proves repeatedly His willingness to call the broken, the lost and the desperate to walk with him and carry out his Kingdom purpose. In Caleb's case, he was born into captivity.

We know this from the time line of the Exodus from Egypt and the age of Caleb when he was included in the party of spies that Moses sent into the Promised Land. The greatest fear of Egypt—including the new pharaoh—was that the Hebrew children were increasing in number. So, shrewd taskmasters were placed over the people with a mandate to make Hebrew life miserable. The Bible does not go into much detail, save that increased toil and labor brought a bitterness that caused the people to cry out to the Lord. Yet the goal of the harsh treatment would seem to be not only controlling the population through fear, but decreasing it through hardship. The Hebrew women were worked hard enough to cause miscarriage, sickness and death. The men were pushed to exhaustion, illness, despair and depression. Those who survived this living torture faced the mandate of killing their first-born male children through late-term abortion. This continued for generations.

I realize most of my readers have not experienced such

circumstances. However, we have all been birthed under a death sentence through the fall of man and introduction of sin into the world, finding ourselves deposited into a world system designed to separate us from our destiny. Caleb had a destiny—a purpose before him. We also have a destiny and purpose before us. It is not just special people whom God ordains to walk out His desires; it is common people like you, me, and Caleb who are called for amazing things. When it comes to God, the ordinary becomes the extraordinary.

> *26 For consider your calling, brethren, that there were not many wise according to the flesh, not many mighty, not many noble; 27 but God has chosen the foolish things of the world to shame the wise, and God has chosen the weak things of the world to shame the things which are strong, 28 and the base things of the world and the despised God has chosen, the things that are not, so that He may nullify the things that are, 29 so that no man may boast before God.*
>
> 1 Corinthians 1:26-29

Paul reminds us that God does not consider birthplace or pedigree as qualifications to walk in relationship with him. Caleb's name in Hebrew meant "dog." Does it get any worse than that? Personally, Caleb's humble situations, surroundings and upbringing give me hope and assurance that we serve a God who loves us, and that the only qualification we need is to receive His love through a relationship with Jesus.

Somewhere in his dark upbringing under the oppressive yoke of Egypt, suffering through toil, hardship and constant threat of death, Caleb found God and God found Caleb. As an enslaved "dog," the odds of a long life were not good. Yet out of these circumstances, Caleb rose up to lead others in victory. Thousands of years later, his story still affects us.

The biblical description of Caleb does not mention any unique physical attributes that qualified him for reward or acclaim. The Bible only says six times that Caleb served God *wholeheartedly*. Thus the qualifier for this mistreated "dog" to become an amazing man of God was found within; it was his decision to position his heart fully towards God.

We can make the same decision today. Positioning ourselves towards God *wholeheartedly* will bring a dynamic shift in our thinking, seeing and living.

My hope in this devotional is to share fresh insights that help you in your journey with God. I pray you are encouraged and challenged. Enjoy *Wholehearted—Crossing Over.*

1

See Things Differently

"But My servant Caleb, because he has had a different spirit and has followed Me fully, I will bring into the land which he entered, and his descendants shall take possession of it.

Numbers 14:24

The people stood on the brink of taking the land God promised them, knowing that battle was coming. Uncertainty and fear coursed through Israel as the sons and daughters of slaves prepared for the greatest challenge to face their fledgling nation. A decision had been made to send key men from each tribe first. Caleb was one of the chosen, along with Joshua.

From the moment of birth, life had been difficult for Caleb, especially since he was considered a gentile. His mother was from the tribe of Judah, but his father was a Kenizzite —a tribe of nomads that moved through the Sinai and the southern part of Palestine. Perhaps it was Caleb's unique heritage that knit his heart in hope with the promise of God for his own land and heritage. Yet Caleb's life of following God and serving God positioned him to be one of the first to step into this promise.

Wholehearted - The Crossing

Israel was ready for their new destination but tension was rife among them. Rumors spread of fortresses and fierce barbaric people. The land they gazed upon was both promising and foreboding, yet inside Caleb's heart and spirit there was a stirring of faith mixed with anticipation. Looking at the men around him, he could not understand their trepidation, the undercurrents of doubt and confusion that weakened them. He saw things differently; he had a different spirit.

The first key we find in the life of Caleb is that in serving God wholeheartedly, he was granted a godly perception—one that is available to all who serve God fully! Sadly, this perception does not extent to all men, as the scripture tells us:

> ...but just as it is written, "Things which eye has not seen and ear has not heard, and which have not entered the heart of man, all that God has prepared for those who love Him."
>
> 1 Corinthians 2:9

So, is it God's desire that we do not see, hear, or conceive all that he has for us? Or is this a prophetic description of men who do not walk with God wholeheartedly? I will leave it to your interpretation, but I do believe that God desires us to walk at a greater level of awareness for the sake of those around us. Being wholehearted qualifies us to see in a new way.

In following God fully, both Caleb and his friend Joshua were given insight—an ability to see with eyes of faith that is essential to each of us in our walk with God. Because of this perspective, invading the land of giants, fortresses and warrior tribes was exciting for them. They saw things differently than those around him, and so they acted differently. Once again, the only qualification

See Things Differently

recorded for this kind of confidence and insight is to fully serve God.

I am convinced that we were created with an ability to see spiritually like no other creature that walks the earth. Somewhere inside each of us is an awareness of innate ability, a hunger, an inner realization, whether acknowledged or not, that there is always something more to see. Consider the example of Elisha's servant.

> *[15] Now when the attendant of the man of God had risen early and gone out, behold, an army with horses and chariots was circling the city. And his servant said to him, "Alas, my master! What shall we do?" [16] So he answered, "Do not fear, for those who are with us are more than those who are with them." [17] Then Elisha prayed and said, "O Lord, I pray, open his eyes that he may see." And the Lord opened the servant's eyes and he saw; and behold, the mountain was full of horses and chariots of fire all around Elisha.*
>
> 2 Kings 6:15-17

Notice that Elisha did not pray that God would open *his* eyes, just the eyes of the servant. It would seem to indicate that Elisha was already able to fully perceive both the natural and the supernatural picture of the moment. He had the ability to see what cannot be seen. Elisha—a man who served God fully—had a perception that eluded those around him.

In David, we also see qualities intrinsic to being wholehearted towards God. The rest of Israel saw Goliath as a giant warrior, a mass of intimidation, an obstacle impossible to overcome. Goliath was their nightmare in the flesh, the boogie man recounted around campfires. Yet because David was able to kill both a bear and a lion, he saw in Goliath a target he could not miss!

What gets lost in the narrative of David, however, is the way God trained him to fight. Nowhere else in the Bible do we see a man trained to kill giants using a sling and stones! Bows, arrows and swords, yes. But a sling? That's a shepherd's toy, not the weapon of a warrior. Or so people thought. Serving God wholly set David up to view the challenge of Goliath triumphantly. In like manner, serving God sets us up for the challenges ahead.

The fact is, we often walk at a level far below God's design for us, and whether we admit it or not, it affects not only our own lives but also those around us. Note Paul's words to the church in Corinth.

For we know in part and we prophesy in part;

1 Corinthians 13:9

Caleb and Joshua didn't see exactly how things would go, but they moved forward with a different vision than their fellow warriors. Wholeheartedly serving God gives us a Kingdom perception for our families, communities and churches; for business in the marketplace; for leadership in education and governmental institutions. This vision is available and necessary for the expansion of the Kingdom of God, and it is only possible when we walk wholeheartedly in relationship with God. Walk wholeheartedly with God and get ready to see in a new and fresh way!

Here are a few honest questions to ask ourselves.

- Do I really believe God wants me to see in a different dimension?

See Things Differently

- Do I see this in scripture?
- Am I currently walking wholeheartedly in my relationship with God?
- Am I willing to risk completely surrendering my life to God?

We need God's perspective. We need to see things differently for our families, our neighbors, our workplaces, our world. We won't get it walking halfheartedly with the Lord.

Wholehearted - The Crossing

2

Declarations of Faith

"Nevertheless my brethren who went up with me made the heart of the people melt with fear; but I followed the Lord my God fully.

Joshua 14:8

To spy out the Promised Land of Canaan, Caleb and Joshua were accompanied by ten other men described as "brethren." In a word: *brothers*. Enduring the struggle of the wilderness together formed a bond between these men who would later pioneer together the future of Israel. Certainly, there was a bond between them, a familiarity from enduring life in the desert, but trials can either divide or unite people. This is why we see a sharp contrast not only in what they saw but also in what they spoke.

> *27 Thus they told him, and said, "We went in to the land where you sent us; and it certainly does flow with milk and honey, and this is its fruit. 28 Nevertheless, the people who live in the land are strong, and the cities are fortified and very large; and moreover, we saw the descendants of Anak there.*
>
> *30 Then Caleb quieted the people before Moses*

> *and said, "We should by all means go up and take possession of it, for we will surely overcome it."*
>
> *31 But the men who had gone up with him said, "We are not able to go up against the people, for they are too strong for us."*
>
> Numbers 13: 27-28, 30

This divergence of perspective is common today. Have you ever witnessed an event, and when someone else recounts the events, it's different from how you saw it? Wholehearted people see things from God's perspective because a godly perspective flows from their hearts. Even the sound of their voice is different. When Jesus declared *"Lazarus, come out!"* it was a call from death to life, a sound that pierced through the tomb of unbelief. I believe there was such power in his voice that Jesus had to identify Lazarus specifically so only he came to life in that graveyard. That is the power of being wholehearted.

> *A good man out of the good treasure of his heart brings forth good; and an evil man out of the evil treasure of his heart brings forth evil. For out of the abundance of the heart his mouth speaks.*
>
> Luke 6:45 (NKJV)

On the day the spies gave their report to the people, Joshua and Caleb spoke with the sound of faith from a godly perspective—the same sound Lazarus heard. Faith sounds differently. Regrettably, the remaining ten spies did not view things as Joshua and Caleb did, and so they did not speak with the same faith. To make matters worse, the faithless spies were critical and negative, melting the people's hearts and causing them to murmur and prepare to stone both Joshua and Caleb.

Declarations of Faith

There is an important element here. Declarations and actions of faith are usually met with resistance! (Yes, stoning constitutes resistance.) In this case, God's judgment fell upon the people as a result of the bad report and their faithless response. Moses had to intercede for Israel as God was going to disown and dispossess them!

> [11] *The Lord said to Moses, "How long will this people spurn Me? And how long will they not believe in Me, despite all the signs which I have performed in their midst?* [12] *I will smite them with pestilence and dispossess them, and I will make you into a nation greater and mightier than they."*
>
> [13] *But Moses said to the Lord…* [19] *"Pardon, I pray, the iniquity of this people according to the greatness of Your lovingkindness, just as You also have forgiven this people, from Egypt even until now."*
>
> Numbers 14:11-13, 19

So where does speaking from faith come from? In the beginning, Adam heard the sound of God walking in the garden, and then came what we know as "the fall of man."

> [8]*They heard the sound of the Lord God walking in the garden in the cool of the day, and the man and his wife hid themselves from the presence of the Lord God among the trees of the garden.* [9]*Then the Lord God called to the man, and said to him, "Where are you?"* [10]*He said, "I heard the sound of You in the garden, and I was afraid because I was naked; so I hid myself."*
>
> Genesis 3:8–10

Man was originally created to hear the sound of God in His life and respond favorably. The Hebrew word for sound here is *shama*, which has its root meaning in "an undivided attention that brings direction, purpose, fellowship and instruction." The first thing Adam did when he fell was to hide himself from a relationship with God, yet it was the very relationship that gave him life. Adam hid himself from the sound of God—the sound that God was making on *his behalf*! After the fall of man, there has been a consistent strategy from the enemy to keep us from hearing from God. This has engendered fear and a tendency against being able to even hear from God. Consider this passage of scripture and the interaction between Moses and the people.

> [18]All the people perceived the thunder and the lightning flashes and the sound of the trumpet and the mountain smoking; and when the people saw it, they trembled and stood at a distance. [19]Then they said to Moses, "Speak to us yourself and we will listen; but let not God speak to us, or we will die." [20]Moses said to the people, "Do not be afraid; for God has come in order to test you, and in order that the fear of Him may remain with you, so that you may not sin." [21]So the people stood at a distance while Moses approached the thick cloud where God was.
>
> Exodus 20:18–21

Many times, we are content to stand at a distance and let someone else interpret the voice of God on our behalf. Yet the Bible speaks of the importance of process and counsel that comes from hearing from God. We have been created to hear the voice of God for ourselves, and we operate best when we do!

Declarations of Faith

Being wholehearted in fully serving, fully following God enacts a redemptive repair in our hearts and life that allows us to not only hear God, but also to make a consistent sound of faith arising from that hearing. In the story of Joshua, we find that he would linger at the tent of meeting long after Moses had already left. It seems that the lives of Joshua and Caleb were connected relationally to God in a way that impacted their speech! Serving God fully meant that they were hearing God, and that produced a different sound. It was the sound that faith makes; the sound of an overcomer. It was the sound of men who knew that God was with them, had directed them, and had promised them something greater. That awareness carried their hearts over the Jordan long before they were able to cross! Even though Caleb was still on the wilderness side of the river, his heart was already living in the Promised Land!

There are many believers today who sound like the ten spies standing on the cusp of crossing over! Most communication from these followers of Jesus is fear-filled criticism and complaints! We were never created to reproduce that kind of sound! Instead of a negative, anxious, and terrified sound, the world desperately needs the sound of faith.

One of my favorite passages for illustrating is in Isaiah.

> *"The Lord God has given me the tongue of the learned, that I should know how to speak a word in season to him who is weary. He awakens me morning by morning, He awakens my ear to hear as the learned.*
>
> Isaiah 50:4 (NKJV)

There is a weary world that needs to hear the sound of God today, and it only comes to those who will be wholehearted in their relationship with God. You and I may be the very conduit God has chosen to release hope and give people the courage to apprehend all that the Lord has for them.

When Israel rejected the report of Joshua and Caleb, choosing instead to believe the weak, faithless spies, they reaped an unexpected result: 40 years wandering the desert as their generation died off. A major part of that wandering involved continuous setting up and tearing down as Israel camped and traveled. It had to have been an incredibly monotonous existence, and all because of believing a negative report. We know that *"faith comes by hearing"* (Romans 10:17). The fact is that living life without faith is just plain monotonous.

Despite the challenges in his life, we do not find a place where Caleb was ever negative or complaining! I believe that was because Caleb walked in a level of hearing and seeing that kept him above the disappointment. Like Caleb, we can live a life above the disappointment! Not only is it possible in God, it's vital. The apostle Paul wrote, *"pressed but not crushed, persecuted but not abandoned"* (2 Corinthians 4:8). Living above disappointment is only possible with being wholehearted.

I believe Caleb was a servant who continued to served well throughout the time in the wilderness. Why do I believe that? Once again, the Bible says that he "served God fully." We don't know whether he helped with manna collection or walked the boundaries of the camp each day. Perhaps he was on litter patrol? But when you served God, it ultimately means serving his people. And when we serve His people, we serve God.

Unfortunately, when people hear a teaching on serving, they often resist it. They filter the message to mean that Christianity is just about coming to church, working the programs, etc. Certainly,

Declarations of Faith

we do not earn our salvation by works—we are saved by grace—but the fruit of that great salvation *does* translate into works.

So how does it work in our day jobs? Do we actually expect to report to work and do nothing? Do we hope to get paid simply from the grace of our employer or customers? This is not reality, and neither is being a believer in Jesus and not being a servant to His people!

> *[34] "Then the King will say to those on His right, 'Come, you who are blessed of My Father, inherit the kingdom prepared for you from the foundation of the world. [35] 'For I was hungry, and you gave Me something to eat; I was thirsty, and you gave Me something to drink; I was a stranger, and you invited Me in; [36] naked, and you clothed Me; I was sick, and you visited Me; I was in prison, and you came to Me.' [37] "Then the righteous will answer Him, 'Lord, when did we see You hungry, and feed You, or thirsty, and give You something to drink? [38] 'And when did we see You a stranger, and invite You in, or naked, and clothe You? [39] 'When did we see You sick, or in prison, and come to You?' [40] "The King will answer and say to them, 'Truly I say to you, to the extent that you did it to one of these brothers of Mine, even the least of them, you did it to Me.'*
>
> Matthew 25:34-40
>
> *You shall walk after the Lord your God and fear him and keep his commandments and obey his voice, and you shall serve him and hold fast to him.*
>
> Deuteronomy 13:4 (ESV)

Wholehearted - The Crossing

If we are truly disciples, believers and followers of Jesus, we need to be like him!

> [26] It shall not be so among you. But whoever would be great among you must be your servant, [27] and whoever would be first among you must be your slave, [28] even as the Son of Man came not to be served but to serve, and to give his life as a ransom for many."
>
> Matthew 20:26-28 (ESV)

Jesus demonstrated it! God himself came down from Heaven, touched earth and lived what is good, right and pleasing to the Father!

We are created with a God-given principle and code to serve! It's as certain as the law of gravity! The problem is the constant battle over who we will serve! Ultimately, we will serve somebody: God, or other things, or ourselves! Bob Dylan certainly got it right when he wrote:

> *You may be a preacher with your spiritual pride*
> *You may be a city councilman taking bribes on the side*
> *You may be working in a barbershop, you may know how to cut hair*
> *You may be somebody's mistress, may be somebody's heir.*
> *But you're gonna have to serve somebody, yes*
> *You're gonna have to serve somebody,*
> *Well, it may be the devil or it may be the Lord*
> *But you're gonna have to serve somebody.*
>
> "Gotta Serve Somebody"
> Bob Dylan
> Columbia Records

Paul wrote this to the church….

Declarations of Faith

> *For you were called to freedom, brothers. Only do not use your freedom as an opportunity for the flesh, but through love serve one another.*
>
> Galatians 5:13 (ESV)

This challenge is not about coming to church. Indeed, the church is not the building. It is the people who come together and identify as believers in Jesus. *That* is church.

> *They exchanged the truth of God for a lie, and worshiped and served created things rather than the Creator—who is forever praised. Amen.*
>
> Romans 1:25 (NIV)

We must develop clear thinking on what is our service and obligation.

> *⁸ For by grace you have been saved through faith; and that not of yourselves, it is the gift of God; ⁹ not as a result of works, so that no one may boast. ¹⁰ For we are His workmanship, created in Christ Jesus for good works, which God prepared beforehand so that we would walk in them.*
>
> Ephesians 2:8-10

It was not works that saved us. However, the fruit of God's grace through our lives *does* accomplish things. And that is a form of works.

Certainly, there is much work to do, and God seeks those willing to do it. He is a builder laying out a blueprint and then searching for the right framers, craftsmen, and finish carpenters to complete the project. God is at his best when doing the work of repair and restoration in the lives of people. As we serve him wholeheartedly, we become instruments he can use.

Look at the various gifts that were given to the church (people) in Romans, Corinthians, and Ephesians…

> *4 For just as we have many members in one body and all the members do not have the same function, 5 so we, who are many, are one body in Christ, and individually members one of another. 6 Since we have gifts that differ according to the grace given to us, each of us is to exercise them accordingly: if prophecy, according to the proportion of his faith; 7 if service, in his serving; or he who teaches, in his teaching; 8 or he who exhorts, in his exhortation; he who gives, with liberality; he who leads, with diligence; he who shows mercy, with cheerfulness.*
>
> Romans 12:4-8

God does not give us gifts for His sake. He does not personally need preaching, prophesying, teaching or exhorting. He's got all that. Every spiritual gift has been given *to* the people, *for* the people, to equip, bless, heal, disciple and bring to wholeness!

So, for those who confess to being believers but are not part of a local church community, how do you serve God's people if you are not present? And how are you served by others?

As a pastor, I know the reasons people remain unconnected. Many times, it's because of past wounds, disillusionment, or shattered dreams. Others feel modern churches are too institutionalized. Despite the reasons, however, I believe there is no "get out of committing to the local church" card! The early church was vibrant, life-giving and transformational, yet it struggled through many flaws and issues because of people just being people!

Declarations of Faith

There were sharp disagreements, constant course corrections and many of the same challenges we have in today's church culture. They had structure, government and liturgy that they practiced as well. This may be simplistic and strong at the same time, but I believe that if God's people would deal with offenses quickly and biblically every time, and be willing to commit and serve one another, we wouldn't have close to half of confessing believers out of fellowship.

If you are one of these believers, please pray and resolve to commit somewhere. The church needs you and you need the church. Numbers 33 shows us that Caleb and Joshua both were stuck in a situation that was not fair to them—they had to live through the years of Israel's desert wanderings as if they shared the guilt—and yet they served God and his people without complaint.

> *And do not be conformed to this world, but be transformed by the renewing of your mind, so that you may prove what the will of God is, that which is good and acceptable and perfect.*
>
> Romans 12:2

The world's way of thinking is to be self-serving. Serving is God's antidote to that selfishness. But to serve effectively, we must have our minds transformed.

> *"If you continue to remain a spectator, you will become a critic."*
>
> Pastor Matt Studer

Heaven met earth in Jesus, forming the body of Christ that he came to serve. Nothing in life fulfills us like serving God through serving His people. And yes, there is a reward. We are laying up treasure in heaven by modeling what Jesus did on earth.

There are three points to serving;

1. Fulfill God's purposes
2. Destroy selfishness
3. Build relationships

The Church is called to serve:

1. God
2. One another
3. A broken world

Would you decide this year that what comes out of your mouth will build and not tear down? Make it a good report for the people around you—those who love you, look up to you, listen and respond to you: your family, friends, community and church. Finally, make a decision to serve.

To serve God, you must serve people, and in serving people, you serve God. All of this is possible if you serve God wholeheartedly. He will put a new song in your mouth, one that is uplifting, life-giving and of fathomless love. Those who continually tear down, slander, complain, mutter or murmur rarely prosper. The only option for life is to live wholeheartedly for God and allow it to change the declarations of our lives.

Here are a few questions to ponder.

- Are my words filled with faith?
- Does my speech build people?
- Is it easier for me to be negative than to peak redemptive faith?

Declarations of Faith

- Does my heart need repaired?
- How can I deal positively with life's disappointments?

Just as the spies' negative report that effectively killed off a generation, so the things we say have a lasting impact. It's imperative that we speak life—the essence of God that comes from walking wholeheartedly with the Lord.

Wholehearted - The Crossing

3

There is an Inheritance

"So Moses swore on that day, saying, 'Surely the land on which your foot has trodden will be an inheritance to you and to your children forever, because you have followed the Lord my God fully.'

Joshua 14:9

One of the worst bumper stickers I've seen reads: <u>I'm spending my children's inheritance.</u> Why does this bother me? Because God desires and has even directed that an inheritance be made both materially and spiritually. The nation of Israel was crossing into Canaan at the time of Moses' statement above, but it was not just for the present but also the future. The Old Testament is rife with principles of inheritance. The New King James Version (NKJV) alone has over 300 references to *inheritance*—who gets it, how it's handed down and how it's appropriated. Again, it is an inheritance both material and spiritual. Sadly, today's Christian culture is permeated with *"Left Behind"* thinking that leads us to conclude that we are being rescued from the earth any day now. Building and planning for the future takes a back seat to day-to-day-survival while waiting for the big lift. Regardless of how one might view the rapture, this approach certainly doesn't grasp inheritance in a biblical way. And because of that, we don't build and lead in a generational way.

There is a story about the construction of New College Oxford, built in 1379. The builders used immense oak beams—the best building materials around—to support the grand dining hall. However, the builders also understood that in time, insects would be a problem, necessitating the replacement of these beams. So, when the college was built, a grove of oak trees was planted nearby to supply future generations when the beams needed replaced. Of course, it takes decades to grow suitable replacement beams. Therefore, the plan was passed down through generations of foresters who understood their place in the span of time. What an excellent example of preparing an inheritance; an approach to building generationally and sacrificing missing from our churches today.

Before we delve further into the principle of inheritance, however, we need to recognize that following God fully impacts a person now and into the generations to come.

> *Brothers, what we do in life... echoes in eternity.*
>
> Maximus Decimus Meridius
> *Gladiator*
> Dir. Ridley Scott
> Dreamworks, 2000

I come from a broken home. My mother was married and divorced five times. She and my biological father divorced when I was six-months old. She hid us from him until I was almost sixteen. I grew up not knowing my dad or even my given last name. Instead,

There is an Inheritance

I was identified with different step-names, stepsisters, stepbrothers and was basically fatherless in any rational sense. In later years, my mom told a story from when we lived in San Antonio Texas. When I was about three years old, I saw a man walking down the sidewalk and ran out to ask him if he was my dad. I lived with a broken heart most of my childhood.

Yet as of this writing, I've been married for thirty-six years to the most incredible woman I've ever known; we have two grown sons who are in blessed marriages and who serve the Lord in vocational ministry. Surprisingly, I attribute this in part to my spiritual inheritance. Despite my broken family history, my mom was a believer who instilled a love for Jesus. In addition, my grandmother and great-grandfather had a faith in God. Through the troubled times, poor choices and reaping of consequences, something was passed down that anchored me spiritually and ultimately left its mark on my life. Considering our heritage, my sons are at least fifth-generation believers. At some point in their past, there was a grandmother or grandfather praying, seeking God wholeheartedly, and leaving a generational blessing. This principle is why God could say to Abraham: *"in you all the families of the earth will be blessed"* (Genesis 12:3). The apostle Paul told Timothy that the same light he saw in his mother and grandmother was in him.

History shows the impact of one generation's decision and how it affects future generations. When Moses declared to Caleb, *"'Surely the land on which your foot has trodden will be an inheritance to you and to your children forever, because you have followed the Lord my God fully'"* (Joshua 14:9), it was a sound of faith that still affects generations. Why? Because a man made a decision to follow God fully—to be wholehearted.

Wholehearted - The Crossing

Earlier I stated that Caleb's mother was from the tribe of Judah, his father a Kenizzite. The Kenizzites were a tribe of nomads that moved through the Sinai and the southern part of Palestine. As nomads, they never settled down or owned anything that could be passed down. I've met many people like that, even believers who were nomadic, restless and never committed or planted anywhere. This makes the promise God gave to Caleb so much more meaningful. To have his own land, his own heritage to occupy and eventually hand down, must have knit Caleb's heart together with hope. Now there was something to invest in, build on and leave to his children…an inheritance. Like Caleb, being a wholehearted follower of Jesus initiates a lineage of faith that God honors. It's worth it.

> *"For David, after he had served the purpose of God in his own generation, fell asleep…"*
>
> Acts 13:36

Don't fall asleep until you've served your purpose!

Questions to ponder:

- How has my life been impacted by previous generations?
- How will my decisions impact the next generations?
- What decision can I make now that will bless the generations after me?
- Have I fallen asleep in my generation?

4

Live Differently

¹⁰"Now behold, the Lord has let me live, just as He spoke, these forty-five years, from the time that the Lord spoke this word to Moses, when Israel walked in the wilderness; and now behold, I am eighty-five years old today. ¹¹"I am still as strong today as I was in the day Moses sent me; as my strength was then, so my strength is now, for war and for going out and coming in.

Joshua 14:10–11

The Bible never speaks of retirement as a worthy goal or even a reward in life! At least, not a retirement of inactivity.

Pastor David Roper writes this:

> *"Half-hearted men—those who fool around with personal ambition and enterprise and who make retirement their chief end don't comprehend. They wither and die before their time. You see them around every town, dull and dreary old men with nothing to do, sitting on park benches or living on Park Avenue, with that dead look in their eyes-over the hill and*

never on top."

A Man to Match The Mountain

Discovery House Publishers

Caleb's wholehearted service to God affected the quality and quantity of his life well into his old age. And he's not alone. Galileo made some of his greatest scientific discoveries at the age of 73. John Glenn returned to space at 77. Benjamin Franklin helped frame the U.S. constitution at 81. Michelangelo was still producing masterpieces at 89. And Senator Strom Thurmond fostered a family of five children starting at 68. (Of course, his wife Nancy was 25.) You will find some of mankind's biggest contributors were over the age of 50!

> [12]*The righteous man will flourish like the palm tree, He will grow like a cedar in Lebanon.* [13]*Planted in the house of the Lord, they will flourish in the courts of our God.* [14]*They will still yield fruit in old age; They shall be full of sap and very green,*
>
> Psalm 92:12-14

Something about serving God fully changes the way we live! In Mark 5, we find the story of Jesus encountering a demon-possessed man and freeing him from captivity and bondage. He was living in the tombs cut from stone. He was unkempt, filthy and dragging broken chains that failed to restrain him. Faced with the Son of God, the demons controlling the man begged to be sent to a herd of pigs instead of cast into perdition. Jesus agreed and all two-thousand swine rushed headlong into the water and drowned. When the people in the village heard of this, they implored Jesus to leave.

Live Differently

Why did the people do this? Scholars believe (and so do I) that it had to do with their economy and lifestyle being interrupted, since the drowned herd of pigs was a considerable loss. Instead of embracing the miracle of transformation through the testimony of this demon possessed man who now sat clothed and in his right mind at Jesus' feet, they feared that following Jesus would change their life too much. The demon-possessed man obviously needed a change of life, and through an encounter with Jesus, he got it. This man ended up obeying Jesus and living drastically differently.

Earlier I shared the brokenness in which I grew up. It got worse as I aged. Despite my early foundation with Christ, I strayed from God for most of my high-school years. Because of my dream became to be a rock and roll guitar legend, I gave myself to a lifestyle I was never created for. Still, I was going to make it big! Ultimately, I realized it was far below the plans God had for me; it was crazy, destructive and dark. I was the man dwelling in the tombs, unkempt spiritually and wearing broken chains like a badge of honor. I sensed that God was calling me back to a place of intimacy with him, to a place of serving and walking in relationship, but I was reluctant to live differently and surrender wholeheartedly to him. I had met my future wife, Robie, the summer after graduating from high school and she captured my heart. It was love at first sight. Within five minutes, I knew I would spend the rest of my life with her…if she would have me. She had the most amazing voice I had ever heard. She was finishing out her senior year in high school and we talked of marriage. Typically, after a date, we would talk for hours sitting in the car out in front of the house (as long as her father was on the porch). During our courtship, I struggled with a sense that I was not living as God wanted me to. I shared my conviction with her, saying that ultimately, if we were going to spend our life together, she needed to know I was called to walk with Christ. This kind of talk was news to her; she had not been raised in a Christian home. Yet there was a deep conviction within me, a deposit of inheritance trying to break through the sin and darkness and deliver me into a different lifestyle.

Although I was being drawn by the Holy Spirit relationally, it took a while until I was freed. In the meantime, we married, started a rock band and hit the road for a couple years playing concerts, bars, college proms and opening for other larger acts. Living the dream, right? Wrong! We finally came to a point where God's call to us out of that lifestyle and into His was greater than anything that could have held us back. To surrender my life to Jesus and live wholeheartedly, I felt to completely close the old chapter and the old-man nature ruling my life. So I sold all my music gear except an acoustic guitar. I really felt music was over for me and for us. Wrong again! However, having been raised in a conservative church where music was a pipe organ and robed choir, I couldn't see any use for my talents. Then one day, Robie and I accepted an invitation to a church in Portland Oregon. Upon entering the sanctuary, my music heart came alive again. There were electric guitars, drums, even bass guitar. There was hope for a musician in Jesus' church! I found a place for my passion in the Kingdom! This was also a generational link for me. In childhood, my biological father had visitation rights until my mother disappeared with us when I was three. However, I retained vague images of guitars since my dad was a player and singer. In fact, these memories had drawn me to the guitar and music my whole life. Now standing in that church, something dead was being called to life. God opened a door for a new expression of the passion imparted to me.

We eventually became part of a contemporary Christian band

Live Differently

and played around the nation, recording several projects in the journey. In the ensuing years, God has used our music to take us into several nations, leading worship, raising up other worship leaders and encouraging the body. It's interesting to me that my own strength, vision and dysfunction apart from God led us into dark venues with no hope, full of depression, self-medication and self glorification. However, since surrendering to Christ and walking wholeheartedly, God took into His plan the same two people with the same passion and talents, and the world opened up. This did not happen until we stepped into serving God fully!

You too can live differently! If you choose to live fully for God, you may be just beginning! *"The righteous shall flourish like a palm tree, he shall grow like a cedar in Lebanon"* (Psalm 92:12). The word *righteousness* here means to be in "right relationship." Right relationship with God begins with being wholehearted. Although I had some conviction about how I was living, I did not have the power to walk in a new way of life until I made the decision to be wholehearted! Then God supplied the power necessary to live in a new way—to come alive! I would encourage you to have the faith to make the same step.

The people in Mark 5 were so concerned with keeping the life they had that they overlooked the miraculous transformation of a man who had been captive. They did not recognize that they were also captives of a different sort and that the hope of transformation stood before them in the form of Jesus!

Questions to ponder:

- Have I been decorating my chains instead of seeking freedom?
- Am I overlooking the possible miracle of

transformation for fear of losing something?
- Am I at a place where I can make the decision to live wholeheartedly now?

5

We Can Drive Out Giants

> ¹²*Now therefore, give me this mountain of which the Lord spoke in that day; for you heard in that day how the Anakim were there, and that the cities were great and fortified. It may be that the Lord will be with me, and I shall be able to drive them out as the Lord said."* ¹³*And Joshua blessed him, and gave Hebron to Caleb the son of Jephunneh as an inheritance.*
>
> Joshua 14:12–13 (NKJV)

Caleb moved quietly into position with the wind in his face, trying not to alarm the livestock of the tribe they had under surveillance. Bleating goats and sounds of hammers on iron wafted through the air. A rickety old dog with patchy fur and a bald tail paced slowly about the edge of the camp seeking scraps. Smoke from a cooking fire outside a rough lean-to made a lazy spiral into the air. Suddenly an enormous man appeared from the tent holding a crude pot to place on the fire. He was followed by another, even larger man. Each wore a rough tunic with a crude knife tucked inside a goat hair belt. Over the top of the tunic was a sword encased in a leather sheath decorated with symbols and carvings. As the first man placed the pot on the fire, his companion shadowed him holding a massive spear greater than Caleb had ever seen. Caleb quieted a shudder as he realized he was looking at warriors from the Anakim—a tribe of giants inhabiting childhood stories and legends. Except the truth was standing before him. Warlike, fierce and intimidating, this fight was not going to be easy, but God had promised.

Caleb is spying on the Promised Land, preparing to take claim his inheritance. This was the encounter that evoked a bad report from the ten spies that accompanied him and Joshua. I imagine he recalled this scene many times during the forty years that Israel wandered the wilderness. There were probably many sleepless nights during which Caleb burned with desperation to finally cross over into the land that God had promised him and his people. Yet we see his declaration explode in Joshua 14 when he says, *"Now therefore give me this mountain of which the Lord spoke..."* Caleb continues to speak differently because he is wholehearted.

It is telling that although there is a promise of God, there is still resistance both to the promise and to God. It is true even today. Regardless of whether promises or declarations of faith carry us forward, we will always encounter resistance, even as the mountains of our dreams loom before us. Inferring from Caleb's response, his mountain was also on his mind. It wasn't that giants weren't a reality; it was that he chose to focus on the mountain rather than the obstacle. The other issue weighing on him was most likely in the conflicting perspectives among the spies. Ten spies measured the giant men of renown against their own meager physical attributes instead of against God himself. Worse yet, they reported fortified cities with impenetrable walls, forgetting the miracles wrought by the hand of God through Moses in their rescue from Egypt. Our memories of God's faithfulness have a tendency to grow dim in the light of the next confrontation. Instead, those memories should be fanned into flames at the first hint of challenge. In Jeremiah, God tells us: *"'For I know the plans that I have for you,' declares the Lord, 'plans for welfare and not for calamity to give you a future and a hope'"* (Jeremiah 29:11). The word picture we have is of a weaver. God is weaving together thoughts that include the mountains and inheritance of promise for His people.

Here are a couple of different aspects of this principle from scripture.

The first aspect is that God has never promised we would not have to struggle. He said as much when he spoke earlier to Moses about the Promised Land and the resistance.

> [16]*"Go and gather the elders of Israel together, and say to them, 'The Lord God of your fathers, the God of Abraham, of Isaac, and of Jacob, appeared to me, saying, "I have surely visited you and seen what is done to you in Egypt;* [17]*and I have said I will bring you up out of the affliction of Egypt to the land of the Canaanites and the Hittites and the Amorites and the Perizzites and the Hivites and the Jebusites, to a land flowing with milk and honey."*
>
> Exodus 3:16–17 (NKJV)

After the death of Moses, God repeatedly tells Joshua to "be strong and of good courage." The future was in front of them but there was resistance!

The second aspect is that we don't have to do this alone! God says in Hebrews 13:5: *"I will never desert you, nor will I ever forsake you."* This is why God's desire is to put us into community. *"God makes a home for the lonely"* (Psalm 68:6).

We can take courage, knowing we do not face resistance alone. In the early struggles of Israel, the enemies were intimidated by the presence of God in their midst. As well as they should have been! We see in 2 Samuel that David fought more giants that just Goliath, and he did not fight alone.

> *¹⁵Now when the Philistines were at war again with Israel, David went down and his servants with him; and as they fought against the Philistines, David became weary. ¹⁶Then Ishbi-benob, who was among the <u>descendants of the giant</u>, the weight of whose spear was three hundred shekels of bronze in weight, was girded with a new sword, and he intended to kill David. ¹⁷But Abishai the son of Zeruiah helped him, and struck the Philistine and killed him. Then the men of David swore to him, saying, "You shall not go out again with us to battle, so that you do not extinguish the lamp of Israel." ¹⁸Now it came about after this that there was war again with the Philistines at Gob; then Sibbecai the Hushathite struck down Saph, who was among the <u>descendants of the giant.</u> ¹⁹There was war with the Philistines again at Gob, and Elhanan the son of Jaare-oregim the Bethlehemite killed Goliath the Gittite, the shaft of whose spear was like a weaver's beam. ²⁰There was war at Gath again, where there was a man of great stature who had six fingers on each hand and six toes on each foot, twenty-four in number; and he also had been <u>born to the giant.</u> ²¹When he defied Israel, Jonathan the son of Shimei,*

We Can Drive Out Giants

David's brother, struck him down. ²²These four were <u>born to the giant in Gath,</u> and they fell by the hand of David and by the hand of his servants.

2 Samuel 21:15–22

Giants, more giants and descendants of giants. Oh my! It is interesting that contending with giants has been a reality for God's people for thousands of years. We all have "giants" in our lives: addictions, anger, rage, bitterness, lust, wounds. If we are honest, we can usually name them.

I'm reminded of the Mel Brooks movie, *Young Frankenstein*, staring Gene Wilder. The character of Igor, played by Marty Feldman, has a hump on his back. For comedic effect, the hump will be on the right side in one scene and on the left for the another scene. Finally, Dr. Frankenstein mentions that he can remove that hump from Igor's back. His reply? "What Hump?"

This also plays true in our lives. Instead of embracing the transformation that is possible, we decorate, justify or just plain ignore the things God is willing to free us from. God's people have absolute promise, purpose and inheritance as we walk through life, but the pathway is fraught with obstacles, diversions, giants and resistance. At our worst, we can be lazy, half-hearted, selfish, sinful, willful uncommitted and unyielding to God and His Word! (If I left anything out, please fill it in here _____).

Half-hearted men and women will not change the world; they will not please God. Instead, they will be condemned to wandering the wilderness, skilled at departing, roaming and setting up camp again just as we see the children of Israel doing in Numbers 33.

Wholehearted - The Crossing

Caleb's attitude was different. His spirit was different and his words were different. Instead of hiding in fear or lethargy, he set out to confront the resistance before him. When we serve God fully, we drive out giants. We do not fight alone. We contend and win. We focus on the mountains and work through the giants. We see ourselves crossing over into the Promised Land even though circumstances are yet to be fulfilled.

Questions to ponder

- What are the giants in my life?
- Am I focusing on the giants or the mountains?
- How does the resistance in my life take form?
- Am I walking alone?

6

The Land Can Rest From War

> ¹³So Joshua blessed him and gave Hebron to Caleb the son of Jephunneh for an inheritance. ¹⁴Therefore, Hebron became the inheritance of Caleb the son of Jephunneh the Kenizzite until this day, because he followed the Lord God of Israel fully. ¹⁵Now the name of Hebron was formerly Kiriath-arba; for Arba was the greatest man among the Anakim. <u>Then the land had rest from war.</u>
>
> Joshua 14:13–15

The Bible has a lot to say about rest. In Genesis, God rested from his work at creation. A Sabbath rest is also mentioned in Exodus 31:15. God spoke to David regarding his son Solomon and the implications of rest in 1 Chronicles.

> "Behold, a son will be born to you, who shall be a man of rest; and I will give him rest from all his enemies on every side; for his name shall be Solomon, and I will give peace and quiet to Israel in his days."
>
> 1 Chronicles 22:9

Not only was Solomon a man of rest, but this rest influenced the country around him. We need more of a spirit of rest. I've heard people say they have been created for war, and certainly war and tribulation are all around us. It would seem biblical though, that we have been created to operate best in an atmosphere of rest and peace. Peace is an elusive refuge that so many of us desperately seek. We dream of finding a peace in a rustic cabin or an ocean side condo. We seek it in accomplishments, education, vacation or relationship. Maybe the right job or the right house or possibly the newest shiny thing will give us peace. I see people making radical moves, hoping a fresh start will make a difference. In the end, however, most are just diversions or illusions at best. Someone said a long time ago: No matter where you go, there you are.

I heard Pastor Jack Hayford say that while God rested on the seventh day, the book of Revelation speaks of the devil coming to earth in great fury, knowing he has but a short time. Apparently, the devil never rests. *"'There is no peace,' says my God, 'for the wicked'"* (Isaiah 57:21).

No wonder rest is elusive and misunderstood. Wickedness drives it out of us. And yet, rest is vital to our growth. It is the root of restoration. When the land rests, it begins a process of preparing for the next season of fruitfulness. As important as this rest is, we won't find it in books or philosophy, food or drink. It comes from being wholehearted in a relationship with the God who created us for work and called us to rest. The elements of rest are like pieces of a puzzle that fit together after identifying and gathering them. Rest, therefore, is not one element but the sum of many.

We need to rest in worship, privately and corporately. I say privately because if a lifestyle of worship is not cultivated individually, it will not manifest corporately. It is imperative that we find the mountaintop, the prayer closet, or the valley hide-a-way and worship as we have seen modeled by men and women of faith.

Why is it important? Developing into a true worshipper changes things. It transforms our lives and the lives of those around us. I guarantee that the man who has developed a lifestyle of rest and worship is a better husband, father, son and friend than the harried, fretful over-achiever most try to be. He is a better businessman, employer and neighbor, and there is a great peace in his life that affects every endeavor in his life.

Likewise, a woman who has developed a lifestyle of worship is a better wife, mother, daughter and friend. She is able to build her home and businesses, bless her family and impact the atmosphere around her for all who come under her purview. Women by nature are influencers. How effective or redemptive they are depends on developing a lifestyle of worship.

Worship is foundational to our lives. Any picture of heaven we see in scripture shows some aspect of praise or worship. (Think of the 24 elders around the throne in Revelation.) Nothing transforms us quite like worship; it invites God's presence, which is the transforming element in our lives. The Bible says of God: *"Yet you are holy, O you who are enthroned upon the praises of Israel"* (Psalms 22:3).

Paul also writes in Romans:

> *Therefore I urge you, brethren, by the mercies of God, to present your bodies a living and holy sacrifice, acceptable to God, which is your spiritual service of worship. And do not be conformed to this world, but*

be transformed by the renewing of your mind, so that you may prove what the will of God is, that which is good and acceptable and perfect.

Romans 12:1-2

David also speaks of finding that place of rest.

¹He who dwells in the secret place of the Most High Shall abide under the shadow of the Almighty. ²I will say of the Lord, "He is my refuge and my fortress; My God, in Him I will trust." ³Surely He shall deliver you from the snare of the fowler and from the perilous pestilence. ⁴He shall cover you with His feathers, and under His wings you shall take refuge; His truth shall be your shield and buckler."

Psalm 91:1-4 (NKJV)

Most of the hunters and fishermen I know have special places they have explored and found to be fruitful on a consistent basis. These are secret places, guarded and shared only with a few. David is writing about dwelling in that secret place with God. The word "dwell" is used biblically to describe "staying or remaining" and even in the concept of the covenant of marriage. It is a place that you decide to inhabit, where you and God meet to pray and worship.

While individual rest is vital, so also is corporate and communal rest because God desires to gather His people into one rest. As of this writing, I have been married to Robie for thirty-six years. Although I am aware of her presence with a phone call, an email or text, there is a different dynamic when we are face to face. Each form of communication presents her at a different level or dynamic of that presence, but the most intimate is always the best.

The Land Can Rest From War

The psalmist wrote: *"I was glad when they said to me, 'Let us go to the house of the Lord'"* (Psalm 122:1). There is a dynamic to a corporate manifestation that openly shows God's presence in a way that brings rest. Certainly, the consistent study of the Word of God brings rest as well. We get fed, assured, often challenged on our attitudes and actions which lend themselves to peace and rest. Yet, rest can also be found in the company of believers as we share core values, carry collective concerns and walk together in the great purposes of God.

Something in the life of Jesus intrigues me about the pace of life. It seems that his ministry would be so much more effective in today's society with the media and social networking. Yet the Bible says: "But when the fullness of the time came, God sent forth His Son," (Galatians 4:4). His ministry started and finished within about three and a half years. Yet he never seemed to be hurried. Harassed yes, but never hurried. There was a pace of life yielding a peace that indicated Jesus was walking in the rest of God. Like Jesus, we find rest in surrender to God and release of our burdens.

> [28] *"Come to Me, all who are weary and heavy-laden, and I will give you rest."*
>
> Matthew 11:28

We see in the passage from Joshua that Caleb followed God fully and received not only the inheritance of Hebron but the rest from war for his land. Even in the storms of life there is a peace.

Questions to ponder:
- Is there consistent peace in my life?
- What areas of my "land" are in war?
- When have there been times of rest?

Wholehearted - The Crossing

7

Joshua The Crossing

Moving into the New

⁵So Moses the servant of the Lord died there in the land of Moab, according to the word of the Lord. ⁶And He buried him in the valley in the land of Moab, opposite Beth-peor; but no man knows his burial place to this day. ⁷Although Moses was one hundred and twenty years old when he died, his eye was not dim, nor his vigor abated. ⁸So the sons of Israel wept for Moses in the plains of Moab thirty days; then the days of weeping and mourning for Moses came to an end. ⁹Now Joshua the son of Nun was filled with the spirit of wisdom, for Moses had laid his hands on him; and the sons of Israel listened to him and did as the Lord had commanded Moses.

Deuteronomy 34:5–9

Joshua sobbed, his body wracked with grief. Even though he had tried to prepare his heart, the death of Moses still shook him. To some, the encounters of Moses with Pharaoh were stories of legend. To Joshua, they were part of his life. His mentor and father figure was gone, buried by God himself. Even not being able to bury him with honor left a void. Those hands... Joshua remembered the rough hands of a shepherd setting aside his staff and embracing him in obedience to God's command to anoint. He felt so unworthy of the appointment to succeed Moses and lead God's people. Although there was a sense of incredible loss, there was also an incredible presence—the same presence he felt as he lingered at the tent of meeting long after Moses had left. It tempered the uncertainty he had about the future, the incredible responsibility regarding the people that weighed upon him. Joshua knew that morning as he watched Moses journeyed up the mountain that he would never be seen again. Still, it didn't make sense; Moses still walked with strength and purpose. He was keen in his thinking and sight. It was time, though, and Moses had shared as much with him as he headed to his own crossing over, the ultimate land of promise.

Examining the life of Joshua, we can imagine the mix of emotions he must have felt. Native Americans describe someone who passes as having "walked on." In the scripture above, Moses has walked on. God has buried him, and what God buries, no man digs up. There must have been such a finality to Joshua's thinking. The weight of responsibility now rested on him conveying the need of moving into something new—not just for him but for all the people.

It also speaks of the different seasons and transitions of life that we all face. If you look at today's news, you'll see that our world is in desperate need of change. We all sense the discouragement, lack of hope and brokenness. We have a need for crossing over into something new and fresh. We are like the children of Israel stuck on the wrong side of the river, the wrong side of our purpose, the wrong side of our God-promised destiny. We can see the other side and know we belong there, but there is a crossing over required.

The story of Joshua crossing over the Jordan has some amazing keys that can propel us in our journey of being wholehearted. As we experienced in Caleb's life, we will find great examples in the life of Joshua leading to greater depths of Kingdom life and purpose.

How many of us have forgotten what it is to dream or hope? And yet, it doesn't have to be that way. We can live differently; we can live well. Joshua's crossing offers principles that will open doors and enable us to live wholeheartedly.

Modern life is a constant series of transitions and changes. So let's be honest—most people do not handle transition very well. It can be the awkward season of a young adult finally moving out of the home and into the future. It can be the first year of a marriage where your life is no longer your own. It can be a job change or moving to a new address. You would think that as much as we transition, we would get better at it. However, I'm convinced that one of the greatest challenges we face is moving into something new. Even armed with a powerful sense of purpose, we often don't understand how to position ourselves to be successful. This is why studying Joshua makes a huge difference our lives. He is a picture of transition in difficult times. As with Joshua, so with all of us—our entrance to the Promised Land can be delayed by unbelief and lack of trust.

We all need to take stock. How many of God's desires, dreams and promises have been delayed by our doubt, unbelief and unwise choices? From the scripture above, we realize that Joshua had a tough act to follow in the leadership of Moses. In the coming chapters, we will examine the life of Joshua and extract principles vital to advancing in the Kingdom of God.

> *¹Now it came about after the death of Moses the servant of the Lord, that the Lord spoke to Joshua the son of Nun, Moses' servant, saying, ²"Moses My servant is dead; now therefore arise, cross this Jordan, you and all this people, to the land which I am giving to them, to the sons of Israel. ³"Every place on which the sole of your foot treads, I have given it to you, just as I spoke to Moses. ⁴"From the wilderness and this Lebanon, even as far as the great river, the river Euphrates, all the land of the Hittites, and as far as the Great Sea toward the setting of the sun will be your territory. ⁵"No man will be able to stand before you all the days of your life. Just as I have been with Moses, I will be with you; I will not fail you or forsake you. ⁶"Be strong and courageous, for you shall give this people possession of the land which I swore to their fathers to give them. ⁷"Only be strong and very courageous; be careful to do according to all the law which Moses My servant commanded you; do not turn from it to the right or to the left, so that you may have success wherever you go. ⁸"This book of the law shall not depart from your mouth, but you shall meditate on it day and night, so that you may be careful to do according to all that is written in it; for then you will make your way prosperous, and then you will have success.*
>
> Joshua 1:1–8

8

Stop Focusing on the Past

⁵So Moses the servant of the Lord died there in the land of Moab, according to the word of the Lord. ⁶And He buried him in the valley in the land of Moab, opposite Beth-peor; but no man knows his burial place to this day. ⁷Although Moses was one hundred and twenty years old when he died, his eye was not dim, nor his vigor abated. ⁸So the sons of Israel wept for Moses in the plains of Moab thirty days; then the days of weeping and mourning for Moses came to an end. ⁹Now Joshua the son of Nun was filled with the spirit of wisdom, for Moses had laid his hands on him; and the sons of Israel listened to him and did as the Lord had commanded Moses.

Deuteronomy 34:5–9

The passage in Deuteronomy speaks of Israel mourning the death of Moses for thirty days. But note the final phrase: it *"came to an end."* It ended! God also buried Moses and to this day, no one knows where. There are a couple of important symbols here. Joshua knew that Moses was dead—he had been in mourning as well—but God spoke once again to Joshua and reiterated this. Moses is dead! God was emphasizing to Joshua that it was time to move on from the past. Stop focusing on what was. He had to stop being paralyzed by the passing of those who had walked on.

Let's get real for a moment. Aren't we all like Joshua? We are fascinated by death, although we were not created for it. In the beginning, Adam was created to live forever! That is why death is such a shock, even when it's a person who has lived a long, full life and seems to have been around since Noah laid the keel on the ark.

Death is a reminder of our original created state. We slow down and gawk at the latest accident or road kill. So much of our entertainment in movies, games and books have to do with death. Death is a billion-dollar industry! Yet the earth was the most impacted by the arrival of life—the life of God in the human form of Jesus—the sting of death conquered by the resurrection. Yet even in our churches and schools of theology, we find more focus on the cross than the resurrection.

It's time to come alive, move forward and stop considering the past. God spoke to Joshua and reiterated: Moses is dead! This truth alone could set so many people free! It is so easy for the past to grip us, hinder us, define us and ultimately keep us from moving forward even when we know we are not in the right place. What drives us there? It can be bad relationships or hurts and certainly rejections. It can be offenses that have turned into bitterness. Our failures can lead to a fear of faith in stepping out. Even reminiscing about the *good ole days* can entrap us. Sometimes we can get so set in our ways that if God wants to breathe something new and fresh, we reject it!

What does Paul tell us about moving forward?

Stop Focusing on the Past

> *¹³Brethren, I do not regard myself as having laid hold of it yet; but one thing I do: forgetting what lies behind and reaching forward to what lies ahead, ¹⁴I press on toward the goal for the prize of the upward call of God in Christ Jesus. ¹⁵Let us therefore, as many as are perfect, have this attitude; and if in anything you have a different attitude, God will reveal that also to you;*
>
> Philippians 3:13–15

There are three important elements to consider from this passage.

1. We are not perfect! Paul did not regard himself as anything and yet he moved beyond the past and forged into the future. It reminds me of the Star Trek movie *Search for Spock* where the Starship Enterprise was badly damaged from a previous battle, yet in their determination to rescue Spock, they were willing to trust a broken ship to carry them into the unknown. The Bible refers to us as vessels. If we are all honest, we can see a little of us in that starship. We are all marked by battle and brokenness; it defines us and propels us.

The problem is that so many of us are waiting in port to see if the ship will become whole again. My friends: that is not the reality of life! I've found in my own life that in moving forward, God effects repairs on a consistent and continuing basis. Paul was arguably the most profound apostle used by God, and he did not look at the past nor count himself as arrived. Neither should we.

2. We must rule our thought-life. When Paul writes about forgetting those things which are behind, he is speaking about exercising our will to set mental boundaries and think differently.

Wholehearted - The Crossing

It is possible! In Romans 12, we are told to not be *"conformed to the world, but transformed by the renewing of our minds."* There is a powerful partnership at work here. I believe it is a combination of grace in the Word of God and decisions on our part to exercise rule over the way we think.

> [7]*For as he thinks in his heart, so is he. "Eat and drink!" he says to you, but his heart is not with you.*
>
> Proverbs 23:7 (NKJV)

We are also told in 1 Corinthians 14:32 that *"the spirits of the prophets are subject to the prophets."* We are taught to be *"sober-minded as you ought"* in 1 Corinthians 15:34.

Countless people have been mired on the wrong side of the river of purpose, possibly because of the way they dwell on the past and think negatively about themselves. It is frightening how much power that has over us and those around us! For example, God might want to impart wisdom and direction to a husband for the sake of his family, but he can be trapped by his own flaws or inability to allow God to renew his mind and heart. Ultimately, it not only affects him personally but his family as well.

It takes maturity to receive from God. Paul writes about having this mind partnered with maturity. There is a maturation in life that brings useful things. Whether it is farmland developing, an athlete training for contests, or a person striving to lead others, maturity is the goal. In a garden, there is a process of watering, weeding, tilling and fertilization, but the goal is the mature produce. Maturity produces!

> [13]*...until we all attain to the unity of the faith, and of the knowledge of the Son of God, to a mature man, to the measure of the stature which belongs to the*

Stop Focusing on the Past

fullness of Christ.

Ephesians 4:13

I have never known a parent who verbalizes the wish that their children would remain immature. In Ephesians 4, Paul speaks of the ascension gifts: apostle, prophet, pastor, teacher and evangelist. It further states that there is a goal for that gift mix—to grow the church by maturing the people. We need to grow up. By the Word of God and the power in the Spirit of God we can!

Questions to Ponder:

- Am I dwelling on the past?
- Can I see how it has hindered me?
- Have I considered the level of maturity in my own life?
- Do I know the necessary steps for maturity in my life?

Wholehearted - The Crossing

9

No Journey Alone

> *¹Now it came about after the death of Moses the servant of the Lord, that the Lord spoke to Joshua the son of Nun, Moses' servant, saying, ²"Moses My servant is dead; now therefore arise, cross this Jordan, you and all this people, to the land which I am giving to them, to the sons of Israel.*
>
> Joshua 1:1–8

In verse two of this passage, God is commanding Joshua and including *"all this people."* What a contrast to our society today. We live in a culture that is selfish and glorifies the individual. The reality is that the journey and obedience that Joshua walked affected those around him. When a man is obedient to the call of God and moves forward, its impact reaches far. When I am walking in relationship with God, there is an incredible effect on my family, my community and my heritage. And my wife? I don't cross the river without her and I don't watch her cross without me! (I make it a habit never to cross her, period! But that's another subject.)

Here is an example of this principle.

The young married couple quickly exited a movie theater,

pushing through the throng of people around them. As they moved down the sidewalk hand in hand, the cool of the night air enveloped them, carrying the melodious cacophony of small town nightlife in full swing. Many people were behind them by now as they stepped off a curb into the crosswalk. The young husband looked to his left and recognized his younger sister driving the car that had stopped to let them cross. Ah, the joys of a close-knit community. They waved, smiled and continued walking across the street. But something didn't feel right. Glancing to his right, he froze as a car hurled toward them. The couple was halfway across in intersection by now. He knew there was no way for the car to stop. In one motion he grasped his young wife's hand and lunged toward the other side, his momentum committed to pulling them both to safety. To his horror, he felt her hand rip from his as she, in her confusion, pulled away and tried to retreat the other direction. Like a slow motion picture, frame by frame, he saw her finally see the car, turn slowly toward it and put her hands out as if to stop it. The car struck her, lifting her first on the hood and then into the windshield. The driver had been turned around talking to a passenger and had no idea where he was headed. He heard the sickening thud and slammed on the brakes…too late…causing the wife's body to roll back to the hood and onto the street.

That was our story. We were the young married couple. The movie was over and Robie and I were the first to enter the crosswalk with a crowd of people on our heels. I held her hand as we strode out from the sidewalk. Looking to my left, I recognized my sister and waved to her. As we continued, I glanced to my right and realized the driver coming from the other way was going too fast to stop. I tightened my grip on Robie's hand to leap across to safety. She had no idea what was happening, had not seen the other car, and pulled her hand out of mine thinking I was just messing around. I turned thinking she had made it back safely to the other side. She hadn't. The oncoming vehicle was manned by a young man who had stolen the car for a joy ride with some friends. He was looking over his right shoulder as he entered the crosswalk at close to thirty-five miles an hour according to the police. When I turned, I was immediately sickened as I watched Robie face the car and put out her hands as if that would stop it. The bumper struck her just below both knees and carried her body up onto the windshield. When the young man realized what happened he slammed on the brakes. Robie shot off of the car's windshield and was flung to the pavement another thirty feet. The police officers said the brakes were not applied until she was on the hood. Witnesses said it looked like something lifted her off the top of the car and deposited her in slow motion in the road. Miraculously, a small scratch just above one of her eyes was the only injury she sustained. It was a lesson learned for both of us.

Crossing together is a core value! Today, Robie and I rarely walk apart and are certainly connected more firmly when crossing a street or traversing a parking lot. Crossing over into something new is not just for ourselves individually. Yes, as we are obedient to the Word of God, it impacts us personally, but it also impacts our family and others around us. When we are moved with compassion, we are moved to action as well. Many people sense hopelessness and long for "the other side." They often need someone to take them there—to model new behaviors, mentor them and help them move in faith, prayer and action.

I'm reminded of the lame man with four friends that brought him to see Jesus. They had to tear a hole in the roof to get their friend before Jesus. It was their place of crossing; a place of healing.

They brought their friend to where a spirit of repair was at work.

There are people all around us who are lost, wounded, blinded and lame both naturally and spiritually. Crossing over is important individually, but there is a community around us that is stuck on the wrong side of the river as well. They can use us. They need us. We can get there together.

One of the travesties I see in the church today is the lack of community and commitment to the body of Christ. This is the church that Jesus laid down his life to build. When God used men like Abraham, Joseph, Moses and so many others, it was never about a personal journey or a personal crossing. Joshua was not called to a journey of self-actualization. His focus went beyond himself. The letters of Paul display his genuine love for the church and his sacrifice for it. You may be a believer and a follower of Jesus, but if you are not rooted and committed to a local community of believers, you are not realizing your fulfillment as a mature Christian. You need others to help you cross over into something new just as others need you.

> *Then the Lord God said, "It is not good for the man to be alone; I will make him a helper suitable for him."*
>
> Genesis 2:18

God's words in Eden were not just for marriage. We were never created to live life alone, and it's never been God's plan to abandon His people. So why would you?

God spoke to Joshua to "move" and to not do it alone. Apparently, Joshua got the message.

> *"If it is disagreeable in your sight to serve the Lord, choose for yourselves today whom you will serve:*

No Journey Alone

whether the gods which your fathers served which were beyond the River, or the gods of the Amorites in whose land you are living; but as for me and my house, we will serve the Lord."

Joshua 24:15

Questions to Ponder

- Have I considered that my journey with God is about more than just me?
- Who are my "all the people"?
- Am I part of the community of believers?
- Who depends on my spiritual leadership and development?

Wholehearted - The Crossing

10

God-Ordained Things Are Ahead

> ³"Every place on which the sole of your foot treads, I have given it to you, just as I spoke to Moses. ⁴"From the wilderness and this Lebanon, even as far as the great river, the river Euphrates, all the land of the Hittites, and as far as the Great Sea toward the setting of the sun will be your territory.
>
> Joshua 1:3–4

Joshua had not only been mentored by the greatest leader Israel had ever known, but he was also an eye witness to miracles that few men had even imagined. So you wouldn't think God would need to encourage him, but this passage shows that he did. With all Joshua had experienced, God was reaffirming to him the things that were ahead. This passage speaks of an amazing future that God had already designed. Even though Joshua was not yet in possession of the Promised Land, God stated that he had already given it to him.

Notice the differing perspectives. Joshua and the people with him had been trapped, literally and figuratively, by the perspective of the faithless ten spies. But God was speaking to Joshua about the future already done in the mind of God, requiring only the partnership of faith working in Joshua and the people to accomplish it.

> ...but just as it is written, "Things which eye has not seen and ear has not heard, And which have not entered the heart of man, All that God has prepared for those who love Him."
>
> 1 Corinthians 2:9

God-ordained things for our lives already exist in the heart of God. They await our participation to become reality.

I find an incredible mystery in this journey with God. I can't count the times I've considered the will of God, sought the will of God or been asked about His will for others. I've heard people talk ad nauseam about the "will of God," the "permissible will of God," and the "perfect will of God." Honestly, it can be frustrating at times, especially since I'm a father and would welcome my children to ask what my thoughts, plans and ideas were!

A number of years ago, there was a difficult relational distance between my youngest son and myself. He had graduated from high school and was off to college with his big-boy pants packed, when suddenly it seemed that I had lost all my brain matter. If I counseled him to turn right, he would take a left. If I forecast sunshine, he'd open an umbrella. Later, in this fog of independence and growing up, he began occasionally calling to ask for advice. That would make my day! Understanding my own father's heart toward my son, I have to wonder why the will of God for the ordained things in our life seem so difficult to grasp?

God-Ordained Things Are Ahead

Did anyone in the Bible ever struggle with this? King David, perhaps?

> *It is the glory of God to conceal a matter, but the glory of kings is to search out a matter.*
>
> Proverbs 25:2

David is answering the very question of why God is so elusive about the matters before us. In wondering why God's will appears concealed, I finally settled in my heart that it was about pursuit—my pursuit of God. He had already pursued and chosen me, just as he has pursued and chosen every believer. The responsibility of pursuing him is now mine.

The Hebrew word for glory used in the verse above is *kabod*. In some uses, it means "image or standard." The use here means "weight." That speaks of my obligation. We have the weight of responsibility to search and pursue the things God has concealed for my good.

Let me explain further.

I live in a culture where men and women hunt and fish. I once told my wife that men don't wear outfits, and she reminded me that I like to shop at Cabela's Outfitters! She had me there. Consider an expert fly fisherman who has learned to pursue fish. He can read the current of the water, match the hatch of insects, and knows the phase of the moon and its effect on fish behavior. A leader I served with was a fly fishing guide. I once referred to his fly fishing *pole* and he quickly corrected me. *"A pole is what you buy at Walmart, Pastor. This is a quality <u>rod</u>!"* I should have known. *"Your rod and your staff, they comfort me"* (Psalm 23:4). (What was I thinking?)

Consider as well a bowhunter who takes incredible preparation in his pursuit. His technical camouflage clothing is washed and treated with scent-free products and then stored carefully. Various animal calls are practiced and perfected. Other gear and preparations are pursued to perfection. Bowhunters learn to gauge the wind, read the terrain, and pattern the habits of creatures they are chasing. Men that I hunt with know the nuances of the bugle of a rutting bull, whether it is a challenge call or just a location bugle from the top of a ridge. All is done in the name of pursuit.

Obviously, we can also pursue material objects as well. It can be a new truck or house as well as anything with fins or fur. My wife will tell you that when I set my mind on a new vehicle, I research it to death! When I finally go into a car lot, I know more about the product than the salesman!

We have it within us to *pursue*. We have been created by the great Pursuer! Even in the garden when Adam sinned and hid, God initiated the search to find him. And in finding the God-ordained things ahead of us, a pursuit is necessary. The key to pursuing is being wholehearted! God spoke to Joshua clearly about what was ahead; I believe it's because Joshua had already learned to relationally pursue God.

Have you ever thought about two people pursuing each other? At some time, there's bound to be a meeting of the minds! Serving God in a wholehearted manner puts us on a collision course with the God-ordained things ahead of us. I believe Joshua had come to the edge of that river many times, wondering and dreaming about the other side. I'm sure he replayed in his mind things he had seen and the possibilities that had haunted him for forty years living with the deep dissatisfaction of knowing he was on the wrong side of the river. God was now speaking encouragement. *It's not over;*

God-Ordained Things Are Ahead

it's time to move.

There are things ahead for all of us. Living wholeheartedly is a key component of walking into them.

Questions to Ponder:

- How often have you thought: *There must be more*?
- Are you good at pursuing the things you desire?
- Have you wondered what life would be like if you pursued God wholeheartedly?
- What things happened when there was a collision of your pursuit of God and His pursuit of you?

11

The Tent of Meeting

> *⁵"No man will be able to stand before you all the days of your life. Just as I have been with Moses, I will be with you; I will not fail you or forsake you. ⁶"Be strong and courageous, for you shall give this people possession of the land which I swore to their fathers to give them.*
>
> Joshua 1:5–6

God prepared Joshua for leadership by promising that his presence would never leave him, and commanding him to be strong and courageous. As a leader, Joshua realized that the journey was bigger than himself and Caleb alone; it also involved those around them. This was important because fear and negativity was keeping Israel out of the Promise Land and breeding captivity. To lead this people, Joshua had to be proven and tested. There could be no crossing over if he was fearful or anxious.

Fear and anxiety are siblings of sorts, with negativity a close cousin. We find them hanging out together as a devilish trinity leading to captivity and the hindering of what God has placed before us. Of course, I'm not saying that life should be lived without some natural fear. A healthy sense of fear has kept me from doing foolish and dangerous things throughout my life. Further, courage is not the absence of fear, but a virtue that helps us do the right thing despite the circumstances. The Bible says, *"the fear of the Lord is the beginning of wisdom"* (Psalm 111:10). Fear and caution have a balanced place in our lives. I have heard for years : *"There are old pilots and bold pilots, but no old, bold pilots."*

Beyond healthy, life-giving fear, however, there is an inordinate fear and anxiety that hinders the pathways God has placed before us. Anxiety is a killer, both in the natural and the spiritual.

> *It is in vain that you rise up early and go late to rest, eating the bread of anxious toil; for he gives to his beloved sleep.*
>
> Psalm 127:2 (ESV)

> *Say to those who have an anxious heart, "Be strong; fear not! Behold, your God will come with vengeance, with the recompense of God. He will come and save you."*
>
> Isaiah 35:4 (ESV)

> *He is like a tree planted by water, that sends out its roots by the stream, and does not fear when heat comes, for its leaves remain green, and is not anxious in the year of drought, for it does not cease to bear fruit."*
>
> Jeremiah 17:8 (ESV)

The negative fear coming from the ten spies had a devastating effect on the people, as we read in the following account.

[1]*Then all the congregation raised a loud cry, and the*

> *people wept that night. ²And all the people of Israel grumbled against Moses and Aaron. The whole congregation said to them, "Would that we had died in the land of Egypt! Or would that we had died in this wilderness! ³Why is the Lord bringing us into this land, to fall by the sword? Our wives and our little ones will become a prey. Would it not be better for us to go back to Egypt?" ⁴And they said to one another, "Let us choose a leader and go back to Egypt." ⁵Then Moses and Aaron fell on their faces before all the assembly of the congregation of the people of Israel.*
>
> Numbers 14:1-5

The devilish trinity of anxiety, fear and negativity elicited a response that doomed a generation to dying in the wilderness instead of moving forward into God's promised destiny. However, we see that Joshua and Caleb had a different reaction to the challenges that lay before them; they had a different voice that ultimately led to different outcomes for themselves and the people.

> *⁶And Joshua the son of Nun and Caleb the son of Jephunneh, who were among those who had spied out the land, tore their clothes ⁷and said to all the congregation of the people of Israel, "The land, which we passed through to spy it out, is an exceedingly good land. ⁸If the Lord delights in us, he will bring us into this land and give it to us, a land that flows with milk and honey. ⁹Only do not rebel against the Lord. And do not fear the people of the land, for they are bread for us. Their protection is removed from them, and the Lord is with us; do not fear them."*
>
> Numbers 14:6–9 (ESV)

Joshua appealed to people to have courage, to not fear, and to not rebel against God. Prophetically he declared that the inhabitants of the Promised Land not only had their protection removed but also were *"bread for us."* In modern terms, he was promising that *"we are going to eat their lunch"*! This was a totally different reaction than what came from those influenced by the faithless spies. Although Joshua and Caleb were in the same party spying on the land and facing the same images, their reactions were full of faith.

So why was Joshua different? From Exodus, we see that something happened in his life to make a difference. It involved the *"tent of meeting"*—a key component of being wholehearted.

> *⁷Now Moses used to take the tent and pitch it outside the camp, far off from the camp, and he called it the tent of meeting. And everyone who sought the Lord would go out to the tent of meeting, which was outside the camp. ⁸Whenever Moses went out to the tent, all the people would rise up, and each would stand at his tent door, and watch Moses until he had gone into the tent. ⁹When Moses entered the tent, the pillar of cloud would descend and stand at the entrance of the tent, and the Lord would speak with Moses. ¹⁰And when all the people saw the pillar of cloud standing at the entrance of the tent, all the people would rise up and worship, each at his tent door. ¹¹Thus the Lord used to speak to Moses face to face, as a man speaks to his friend. When Moses turned again into the camp, his assistant Joshua the son of Nun, a young man, would not depart from the tent.*
>
> Exodus 33:7–11 (ESV)

The Tent of Meeting

Unlike most of the others, Joshua was not content merely watching Moses have encounters with God. He wanted to have his own encounter, so while the others stayed home, he made a practice of meeting with God.

When we meet regularly with God in prayer, reading his word and immersing ourselves in worship, it changes everything: It changes how we view things; it gives direction to our steps; it changes the sound that comes out of our mouths. It is hard to be anxious, fearful or critical when we are in the tent of meeting. Personally, I find when I'm critical and negative, it's usually because I have neglected meeting with God and his people. Let's face it: We are created for community with God and man.

> ...not neglecting to meet together, as is the habit of some, but encouraging one another, and all the more as you see the Day drawing near.
>
> Hebrews 10:25 (ESV)

There is a prophetic symbolism in the tent of meeting of Joshua's day that applies to modern believers. The people of Israel experienced God's love, power, deliverance and provision, yet we see that there was a tendency to stand at their own tent instead of the tent of meeting.

We live in a Christian culture today that the early church would scarcely recognize. From my informal research inquiring of other Christian leaders, close to fifty percent of believers are not in any sort of church community. This is unfortunate. Jesus came to earth to build his church, knowing that God delights in his people connecting with him and others.

> *I was glad when they said to me, "Let us go to the house of the Lord!"*
>
> Psalm 122:1 (ESV)

I've experienced this issue firsthand. There was a transformation when I surrendered my life to Christ, but another transformation occurred when I committed my life to serve a local church. I realized I could not be just an observer, a fan or admirer of Jesus. As a follower of Christ, I had a responsibility to be in community. Further, being mentored by people who carried the spirit of God had a profound impact my life. Having been raised with broken foundations, I needed to engage with others who were on the same journey. Yes, I committed to spending time in prayer and worship with God alone, but I also found that the gathering atmosphere was necessary. If Jesus was building something, I wanted to be a part of it. If he had a purpose for the body that he laid his life down for, I wanted to be part of that purpose.

I've seen others walk away from the gathering of God's people because it's too religious, too structured, they were offended or just distracted. Sometimes it's the fear of commitment, or reluctance to be accountable, that keeps people out of fellowship. And certainly, it can sometimes be poor leadership. As a committed part of a body, I've been blessed as well as hurt. So what? Families hurt each other at times, yet we seem to measure the church gathering on a different scale.

A pastor friend of mine recently went to Pakistan where he encountered extreme poverty, oppressive living conditions and church services with armed men guarding the building. I will never forget his description of the church in Pakistan. *"You should see the church there; she is beautiful!"* And she *is* beautiful! She is

The Tent of Meeting

filled with failure, flaws and success stories that are moving her forward! She is a testimony of transformed people, regenerated minds, renewed hearts and alive spirits. In the book of Acts, we see that God was constantly adding to the church those who were being saved. God is still calling and gathering people to "the tent of meeting"!

Questions to Ponder:

- Am I committed to a personal tent of meeting time?
- Am I committed to a corporate "tent of meeting" gathering?
- Is it time to revisit my commitment to the Christian Community?

Wholehearted - The Crossing

12

Faith Crosses Rivers

Getting to one of my favorite hunting spots in Idaho requires me to cross a creek. Some years it is easily navigable, and at other times inclement weather turns this benign stream into a raging torrent. I've tried a variety of things to make the crossing easier: large garbage bags over my boots and calves, hip waders like fly fishermen use, even a walking stick to help navigate the slick, moss-covered rocks. Still, nothing removes the danger. One slip into that *creek of crossing* means a wet hike or a broken bone!

Anytime we move forward, we find obstacles that must be forded. Growing up in a farming and ranching community, I learned that the most vulnerable time was when moving livestock from one point to another. Transitions can be the most treacherous of journeys if we are not prepared. It is at those times that we are most exposed, threatened and hesitant…and some never make the crossing at all!

In the continuing story of Joshua, I want to illustrate some things we can apply as we move forward.

> [6]*"Be strong and courageous, for you shall give this people possession of the land which I swore to their*

> fathers to give them. ⁷"Only be strong and very courageous; be careful to do according to all the law which Moses My servant commanded you; do not turn from it to the right or to the left, so that you may have success wherever you go. ⁸"This book of the law shall not depart from your mouth, but you shall meditate on it day and night, so that you may be careful to do according to all that is written in it; for then you will make your way prosperous, and then you will have success. ⁹"Have I not commanded you? Be strong and courageous! Do not tremble or be dismayed, for the Lord your God is with you wherever you go."
>
> Joshua 1:6–9

This interaction between God and Joshua highlights two powerful points to successfully crossing over. First, in speaking with Joshua, God tells him three times to *"be strong and of good courage."* It takes faith to cross rivers. It takes faith to cross over anything. Faith is required to move ahead into our life's purpose and calling. We are created to operate in an atmosphere of faith! Why do I say that? Where do we see that?

> *And without faith it is impossible to please Him, for he who comes to God must believe that He is and that He is a rewarder of those who seek Him.*
>
> Hebrews 11:6

If God's Word states: *"without faith it's impossible to please God,"* then it must be true. God has not created us to fall, fail or displease him! Faith is the culture in which we work best; it is how we move forward and please God.

The enemy would like us to function differently. His plan

attacks our emotions, our relationships, our finances, our decisions, our peace of mind and ultimately our ability to deal with difficult times. He does this by fostering an atmosphere of craven fear—not the healthy fear that leads to wisdom, but a fear leading to death.

Fortunately, God has the antidote.

> *For God has not given us a spirit of timidity, but of power and love and discipline.*
>
> 2 Timothy 1:7

The word *power* used here is the Greek *dunamis*, which means "inherent power." All words derived from the stem *duna* have the basic meaning of being "able and capable."

This speaks of God imparting power to us, making us capable, able men. An environment of fear changes when men of God are present! God spoke something powerful into Joshua because fear had locked Israel in the wilderness side instead of releasing them to the future God had promised. In response to everything God wants to do, the enemy creates a counter-culture of fear to prevent us from doing it.

Deeply entrenched fears become phobias so ingrained with our personality that they feel normal, a part of us we can't imagine living without. The result is a form of fear which storms our mind and shakes our confidence, robbing us of the courage to face challenging situations. Not surprisingly, modern science has been able to classify hundreds of common phobias afflicting mankind.

> *Phobic individuals are so often inundated with anxiety that they start avoiding feared objects or situations.*
>
> *In trying to analyze how many phobias are there, you*

> *must understand that phobia is broadly classified into three distinct groups and there are hundreds of specific identified phobia conditions under each group. This list grows everyday as the world of medical science improves and finds remedy.*
>
> Jan Heering
Master Coach, Psychological Trainer and Author
Founder and President of the Morpheus Institute

Fear is the enemy of faith just as faith is the enemy of fear.

Let's look again at the different reactions among the twelve men that Moses sent into the Promised Land and see how faith and fear played a role.

> *¹ The Lord spoke to Moses, saying, ² "Send men to spy out the land of Canaan, which I am giving to the people of Israel. From each tribe of their fathers you shall send a man, everyone a chief among them."*
>
> Numbers 13:1-2 (ESV)

> *¹⁷ Moses sent them to spy out the land of Canaan and said to them, "Go up into the Negev and go up into the hill country, ¹⁸ and see what the land is, and whether the people who dwell in it are strong or weak, whether they are few or many,*
>
> Numbers 13:17-18 (ESV)

> *²⁵ At the end of forty days they returned from spying out the land. ²⁶ And they came to Moses and Aaron and to all the congregation of the people of Israel in the wilderness of Paran, at Kadesh. They brought back word to them and to all the congregation, and showed*

them the fruit of the land. ²⁷ *And they told him, "We came to the land to which you sent us. It flows with milk and honey, and this is its fruit.* ²⁸ *However, the people who dwell in the land are strong, and the cities are fortified and very large. And besides, we saw the descendants of Anak there.* ²⁹ *The Amalekites dwell in the land of the Negeb. The Hittites, the Jebusites, and the Amorites dwell in the hill country. And the Canaanites dwell by the sea, and along the Jordan."* ³⁰ *But Caleb quieted the people before Moses and said, "Let us go up at once and occupy it, for we are well able to overcome it."* ³¹ *Then the men who had gone up with him said, "We are not able to go up against the people, for they are stronger than we are."* ³² *So they brought to the people of Israel a bad report of the land that they had spied out, saying, "The land, through which we have gone to spy it out, is a land that devours its inhabitants, and all the people that we saw in it are of great height.* ³³ *And there we saw the Nephilim (the sons of Anak, who come from the Nephilim), and we seemed to ourselves like grasshoppers, and so we seemed to them."*

Numbers 13:25-33 (ESV)

Because of ingrained fear, the people had developed several new phobias: Hittite-phobia, Caanite-phobia, Jebusite-phobia. If only God had sent psychoanalysts! Fear not only changes the way we look at every situation, but it changes the way we view ourselves! The ten fearful spies looked upon themselves in a totally different way than how they had been created to be. In an atmosphere of fear, the outward view and the inward view are both clouded and nearly impossible to separate.

Now in contrast, look at the report of Joshua & Caleb...

> *⁶ And Joshua the son of Nun and Caleb the son of Jephunneh, who were among those who had spied out the land, tore their clothes ⁷ and said to all the congregation of the people of Israel, "The land, which we passed through to spy it out, is an exceedingly good land. ⁸ If the Lord delights in us, he will bring us into this land and give it to us, a land that flows with milk and honey. ⁹ Only do not rebel against the Lord. And do not fear the people of the land, for they are bread for us. Their protection is removed from them, and the Lord is with us; do not fear them."*
>
> Numbers 14:6-9 (ESV)

Where the other spies made the hearts of people melt with the report of fear, Joshua and Caleb saw nothing but promise and prosperity. As we have been asking throughout this study, why did they see things so differently?

Here are a couple of observations from this passage in Numbers.

In the report of the ten spies, there was no mention of God. But in the report from Joshua & Caleb, God was referenced three times. That is significant! Even though the situation was the same—same mountains, giants and other obstacles, when God was admitted into the picture, things changed. Yes, God instructed Moses to select leaders of the tribes, yet of the twelve selected, only two referenced God in their assessments. Somewhere along the line, those leaders had missed the tent of meeting! Those leaders did not have a relationship with God leading to a faith-filled, victorious paradigm.

Faith Crosses Rivers

Fear keeps us from crossing over into:
- healthy relationships
- witnessing about Jesus
- making commitments
- gathering with the body of Christ
- building for the future
- giving ourselves to worship
- developing Intimacy with our spouse
- starting new ministries
- believing for the extraordinary

The unfortunate thing is that their lack of faith and ensuing phobias condemned not only themselves but their families as well. My family needs a husband, a father, a grandfather and a leader who has a relationship with God and walks in an atmosphere of faith. It is absolutely critical for them that I serve God faithfully.

When I walk in faith and eschew fear, it affects everything. My outlook on situations changes. I view myself and others differently. When I am in vibrant relationship with God through worship, prayer, devotion and fellowship, my family takes notice! And when those components come together, they form an invitation to faith. *"Faith comes by hearing..."*

My relationship with God grows my faith and gives me what it takes to cross the next obstacle in the journey, even if it's a pair of hip waders or possibly a log bridge!

> *I sought the LORD, and He answered me, and delivered me from all my fears.*
>
> Psalm 34:4

Wholehearted - The Crossing

This speaks so powerfully of relationship. In the seeking of God, there is an antidote for fear.

God spoke to Joshua three times as he was about to cross over into the future of promise. *"Be strong and of good courage."* Like Joshua, you and I were created to operate in an atmosphere of faith. There is a lot of life before us. I want to enter into that future with faith and not fear. How about you? Let's do it together.

Questions to Ponder:
- What have I done in life based on fear?
- What have I done in life based on faith?
- How do I receive faith?

13

Word Up!

> *⁷ Only be strong and very courageous, being careful to do according to all the law that Moses my servant commanded you. Do not turn from it to the right hand or to the left, that you may have good success wherever you go. ⁸ <u>This Book of the Law shall not depart from your mouth</u>, but you shall meditate on it day and night, so that you may be careful to do according to all that is written in it. For then you will make your way prosperous, and then you will have good success.*
>
> Joshua 1:7-8 (ESV)

Joshua now faced a greater challenge than giants or rivers. He was preparing to move God's people and his own family forward into an ungodly culture. As many times as we have heard this story taught, I'm not sure we fully consider the spiritual ramifications of the ungodly environment that lay before them—various cultic expressions of worship and devilish faith. Instead, we typically focus on the battle ahead, the march around Jericho and the overtaking of various enemies stupid enough to stand in God's way—the stuff that makes blockbuster movies.

Tragically, I've seen people make life-changing decisions to uproot themselves, selling out and moving on because of job opportunities or family distress—the "grass is greener" syndrome—without considering the spiritual environment ahead of them. I typically counsel people to investigate the spiritual climate as well as the housing market, the job market, and the cultural scene. For example, if there are two colleges that meet the educational needs they are looking for, look for churches in the area that are healthy and vibrant. It takes courage to live as a Godly person in our culture!

Joshua was taking the people into a new environment and they needed preparation! We find in verses 10-11 that part of this preparation included a march of the armed men through the camp to instill courage in the people.

> *10 And Joshua commanded the officers of the people,*
> *11 "Pass through the midst of the camp and command the people, 'Prepare your provisions, for within three days you are to pass over this Jordan to go in to take possession of the land that the Lord your God is giving you to possess.'"*
>
> Joshua 1:10-11 (ESV)

Notice that in preparation for this momentous journey, God's most important instructions were for preparations *before* the march occurred, prior to the assembling of the people of Israel.

There is a huge difference between the way that I assemble things and the way my wife does. She is meticulous and plans her steps. I prefer to "wing it." Of course, her plans usually work

Word Up!

to perfection whereas I usually have parts left over to add to my bucket of "extra's" in my shop. Maybe if I read the instructions first...?

Many people are crossing over into the most important season in their life—the future—without proper assembly or preparation. It's like:

- driving through a long tunnel without lights
- hiking in the wilderness without a map
- boating in thick fog
- jumping from a plane and wondering if you packed your chute.

As we prepare for action, we must treat the most important parts of our plan with the highest priority. Perhaps this is why God spoke to Joshua regarding his Word being paramount.

> *This Book of the Law shall not depart from your mouth, but you shall meditate on it day and night, so that you may be careful to do according to all that is written in it.*
>
> Joshua 1:8

Word UP!

You and I were created to walk in an adventurous relationship with God; to cross over into new things; to cultivate and reap in new seasons. Yet we cannot do this without faith. We were created to operate in the atmosphere of faith, not of fear. *"Without faith it's impossible to please God"* (Hebrews 11:6). Fear binds us, but faith frees us. When we operate in faith, life just works better! Our relationships flourish in an atmosphere of faith. We cross over by faith, take chances by faith, reach new heights by faith. Romans

10:17 tell us, *"faith comes by hearing, and hearing by the Word of God."*

> *¹ Now faith is the substance of things hoped for, the evidence of things not seen. ² For by it the elders obtained a good testimony. ³ By faith we understand that the worlds were framed by the word of God, so that the things which are seen were not made of things which are visible.*
>
> Hebrews 11:1-3 (NKJV)

These words get me fired up. I need more faith—the faith that only comes by hearing the Word of God. It comes from reading, teaching and remembering the stories of men and women who moved in faith, not fear! I urge you to continue in Hebrews 11 on your own. It is sometimes called the "Hall of Faith" chapter. I want to be included in a "Hall of Faith," not a "Hall of Fear." We are believers created for the plans of God. The future is before us and God *is* with us.

There are rivers to cross in life, promises to obtain and things to be assembled that don't work without following the directions. However, in our preparation for life, the Bible is so much more than just instructions.

- It is informative and historical, offering wisdom that applies to our lives.
- It is mystery and the answer to mysteries.
- It is the past, present and future all in one.
- It brings detection, correction, comfort and challenge.
- It reveals miracles and gives hope.
- It takes the fears and uncertainties of today and turns

them into faith for tomorrow.

- Its helps a man become a better husband, father and neighbor.
- It brings answers to questions not yet asked.
- It reveals the glory and passion of God.
- It colors our world.
- It is not just instruction although it contains plenty.
- It is the story of heroes and failures and ordinary people used to do extraordinary things.
- It was in the beginning with God and it is God.
- It is both practical and supernatural.
- It is at times hard to understand; we need the help of Holy Spirit to appropriate it in our lives.
- It washes us, changes us and transforms our thinking.
- It reveals the judgment of God and the grace of God.
- It is living, active and sharper than any two-edged sword.
- It is relational.

When God spoke to Joshua,

> *⁸ This Book of the Law shall not depart from your mouth, but you shall meditate on it day and night, so that you may be careful to do according to all that is written in it. For then you will make your way prosperous, and then you will have good success.*

God was speaking of instruction but also of relationship and empowerment—all the things Joshua would need to focus on God when he faced giants, obstacles and rivers. God wanted Joshua to be reminded of the love of God—the divine resource available to him out of relationship. In all that he faced, Joshua needed to remember that God was with him!

God was in essence saying, "I've got this as you move forward."

> ¹ *Blessed is the man who walks not in the counsel of the wicked, nor stands in the way of sinners, nor sits in the seat of scoffers;* ² *but his delight is in the law of the Lord, and on his law he meditates day and night.* ³ *He is like a tree planted by streams of water that yields its fruit in its season, and its leaf does not wither. In all that he does, he prospers.*
>
> Psalm 1:1-3 (ESV)

The Word of God revealed through the Bible is about God's pursuit of mankind for relationship. Unfortunately, many of us try to cross the rivers on our own, sans God and his Word. I have learned over time that being in relationship with God is the most vital thing in my life. Many Christians are crossing over into new dimensions of life without proper preparation.

> ¹ *In the beginning was the Word, and the Word was with God, and the Word was God.* ² *He was in the beginning with God.* ³ *All things were made through Him, and without Him nothing was made that was made.* ⁴ *In Him was life, and the life was the light of men.* ⁵ *And the light shines in the darkness, and the darkness did not comprehend it.*
>
> John 1:1-5 (NKJV)
>
> *And the Word became flesh and dwelt among us, and*

Word Up!

we beheld His glory, the glory as of the only begotten of the Father, full of grace and truth.

John 1:14 (NKJV)

The *Word* in this verse is Jesus. Are you crossing over into the future without knowing him? If so, I wholeheartedly recommend you reconsider.

Questions to Ponder:

- Do I consider the spiritual environment of any transition?
- How do I prepare spiritually for life changes?
- How important is the Word of God in my life?

Wholehearted - The Crossing

14

Positioning to Pursue

¹ Then Joshua rose early in the morning and they set out from Shittim. And they came to the Jordan, he and all the people of Israel, and lodged there before they passed over. ² At the end of three days the officers went through the camp ³ and commanded the people, "As soon as you see the ark of the covenant of the Lord your God being carried by the Levitical priests, then you shall set out from your place and follow it. ⁴ Yet there shall be a distance between you and it, about 2,000 cubits in length. Do not come near it, in order that you may know the way you shall go, for you have not passed this way before."

Joshua 3:1-7 (ESV)

The ark of the covenant represented the presence of the Lord, and its position with respect to Israel was vital to their success as a nation. The same is true today. The positioning of God in our lives is extremely critical! Consequently, I teach a lot about positioning. As an athlete and later a coach, the difference between winning and losing usually came down to someone being in the right position at the right time. It was interesting that even with a mature varsity athlete, the difference in play, both defensively and offensively, had to do with correct positioning. If a good shooter was going through a slump, for example, I studied his footing and alignment; this usually led me to where his fundamental mechanics had failed.

As a young man, I became a horse trader of sorts when it came to buying and selling cars. I had some really nice ones, but never enough money to keep them all. So I would buy one and fix it up, then sell it to get another one. Because I was a minor, thus not able to legally own a car, my mom put them all in her name. One day she got a letter from the Department of Motor Vehicles stating that if she purchased one more car this year, she would have to get a dealer's license! Through this early childhood education, I learned a lot about positioning (and a little about the law). My wife can attest to the fact that I can tell by the way a car is sitting in a field, yard or street, whether it is for sale or not, even from half a mile away.

Many aspects of life are about positioning, including our relationship with God.

In our scripture above, as the people of Israel prepared to move forward, the officers went through the camp giving specific instructions for their positioning.

> *³ and they commanded the people, saying, "When you see the ark of the covenant of the Lord your God, and the priests, the Levites, bearing it, then you shall set out from your place and go after it.*
>
> Joshua 3:3 (NKJV)

Positioning to Pursue

Positioning as described here, is in the natural—the people were to be outside their tents ready to go—but also speaks of the spiritual dimensions. The most critical steps we make as we move into the future involve making sure we have positioned ourselves within God's will to pursue and follow him—not in front of him and certainly not apart from him! I've found in crossing over into something new, I must first examine the fundamental place that God has in my life. Am I making *my* plans and then asking God to bless them? Or am I holding onto them loosely and allowing God to mold them? Have I started out by simply asking God to formulate my plans and steps, or am I truly seeking his will?

Of course, as a human being endowed with a free will, I understand the incredible freedom I have in my choices. Yet, if I am positioned relationally with God, I find that dreams, ideas, plans and conclusions are dropped into my heart by his Spirit. In this awareness, I can confidently move forward knowing God will bring a course correction to my life at any time. At other times, however, when I have bigger decisions to make—decisions that possibly impact my family—I slow down the process, positioning myself to be more deliberate about discerning God's direction. Positioning also deals with pride and humility. The Bible says, *"God opposes the proud but gives grace to the humble"* (James 4:6). I have learned that positioning myself in humility leads to far more victorious living than positioning in pride.

> *The mind of man plans his way, But the Lord directs his steps.*
>
> Proverbs 16:9

The steps of a man are established by the Lord, and He delights in his way.

Psalm 37:23

...and they commanded the people, saying, "When you see the ark of the covenant of the Lord your God, and the priests, the Levites, bearing it, then you shall set out from your place and <u>go after it.</u>

Joshua 3:3 (NKJV)

Men, in their "hunter-gatherer" persona, can get caught up in the pursuit of something to their detriment. It's part of who we are. The problem comes when we pursue things that God never intended for us to have, at least at the time of our striving. It is easy for us to get ahead of God, which is nearly as bad as falling behind him.

Questions to Ponder:

- Do I understand the importance of positioning myself?
- When have I positioned myself before God and seen the fruit of it?
- Can I imagine a life of pursuing God?

15

Made To Be Different

⁵Then Joshua said to the people, "Consecrate yourselves, for tomorrow the Lord will do wonders among you."

Joshua 3:5 (ESV)

Consecrate yourselves can sound like a complicated spiritual command that goes over the heads of most folks. I know it did mine for the longest time. In reality, to *"consecrate"* is a straightforward concept when we look carefully at the definition.

CONSECRATION - Separation of persons, utensils, buildings, or places from everyday secular uses for exclusive dedication to holy or sacred use. [1]

To put it simply: We were made to be different!

I can't tell you exactly when this understanding exploded in my thinking, but it changed everything. I was made to be different. I could live "up and not down." I could commit to God all of my gifting, abilities and passions! I love to hunt, play music and tinker with old cars. That's me! That's who God created me to be so I can

---
1 Elwell, W. A., & Comfort, P. W. (2001). *Tyndale Bible dictionary.* Tyndale reference library (310). Wheaton, IL: Tyndale House Publishers.

serve him!

Of course, we all have gifts and abilities, talents and potential. Just as a kitchen has regular dishes and company dishes, we have various tools and instruments for different jobs and endeavors. We have work clothes and office clothes. Clothes for the woods and clothes that are just comfortable. Some of my favorite clothes are not allowed out of the house by Robie! As a musician, I've accumulated a number of guitars, each of which serve a different purpose depending on the project at hand. Every one has a consecrated purpose, a unique sound and playability.

Before I came into this revelation, however, I was at a point in life where I set aside my instruments for service to God. In recommitting my life to God, I also abandoned my music because it elevated my heart in a wrong way. Ultimately, God called me back to music to serve him, but the gifting, passions and resources that music entailed were now consecrated to God! It was a determination I had to make!

In the scripture above, Joshua told the people to consecrate themselves because they had been set apart for the Lord. Notice also that this is not something Joshua could make them do; rather, it was a determination of their free will—a *life-changing decision* on their part. The same decision today is more than just trying to add some God-things to our life or putting on a Jesus shirt. It is about making a covenantal decision to set our life apart in service to God.

When I learned to consecrate my life to God, it completely changed how I viewed myself. I realized that I had been living my life outside of its intended purpose. (This is also one of the definitions of abuse. A screwdriver is not a hammer.) We have been created to walk in a relationship with the living God, to live a lifestyle of worship and service. Anything outside of that is not our intended purpose.

C.S. Lewis wrote, *"I was not born to be free, but to adore and obey."*

As we learn to consecrate our lives, we begin functioning differently. Our decisions, perspectives, passions and core values change as we realize there is a grander purpose for our lives. Our values—whatever they may be—influence how we function. For example, if we have a core value of eating healthfully, it will obviously influence how we eat! If, as a believer, we have a core value of righteousness, meaning *"to be in right relationship,"* then we will struggle with actions, attitudes and decisions that are outside of that core value, whether in the context of our relationships, our work or our recreation. Consecration is more than realizing we are called to be different; it is making the decision for our lives to be set apart in relationship with God. When we do this, we set ourselves up for wonders!

> *Then Joshua said to the people, "Consecrate yourselves, for tomorrow the Lord will do wonders among you."*
>
> Joshua 3:5 (ESV)

In consecrating ourselves, we not only view ourselves differently, but we position ourselves in the pathway of a supernatural God who does amazing things. *"Wonders"* is how Joshua framed it! And he had seen wonders! He had seen the water from the rock, the provision of manna, the plagues released against the captivity of Egypt, and the parting of the Red Sea.

Wonders and purposes await as consecration sets us up to be used in the capacities that God has planned for us. We were created to walk, participate, receive and rejoice in these wonders. Making a decision to consecrate ourselves and set apart our lives is the key to entering into all God has in store for those who love him!

Questions to Ponder:

- How do I view myself now?
- Am I ready to consecrate myself?
- Has it been a while since I experienced the wonder of God?
- What is keeping me from taking this step?

16

Made for Promotion

> *⁷ The Lord said to Joshua, "Today I will begin to exalt you in the sight of all Israel, that they may know that, as I was with Moses, so I will be with you.*

The word *"exalted"* here means, "advanced or promoted." When God leads us into new things, we often experience advancement that glorifies God. Those around us can also see that God is real, powerful and effective.

You and I have been created with a desire to advance—a spiritual mandate that needs to be understood before we can fully act upon it. In Genesis 1, we find a key.

> *²⁶Then God said, "Let us make man in our image, after our likeness. And let them have dominion over the fish of the sea and over the birds of the heavens and over the livestock and over all the earth and over every creeping thing that creeps on the earth." ²⁷So God created man in his own image, in the image of God he created him; male and female he created them. ²⁸And God blessed them. And God said to them, "Be fruitful and multiply and fill the earth and subdue it, and*

> *have dominion over the fish of the sea and over the birds of the heavens and over every living thing that moves on the earth."*
>
> Genesis 1:26–28 (ESV)

Then we see another reference in Genesis 2.

> *5 When no bush of the field was yet in the land and no small plant of the field had yet sprung up—for the Lord God had not caused it to rain on the land, and there was no man to work the ground,*
>
> Genesis 2:5 (ESV)

It is amazing to me in the conception of creation that God, even before he rested, created man and appointed him to steward the earth. That is promotion! In fact, Genesis 2 speaks of things not yet set into motion because there was no man to work the ground! From the very beginning, there was instilled in man a sense of purpose—a desire to advance and excel. As members of the human race, it was intended for you and me as well.

We see it in the young boy who agonizes on the bench, hoping the coach puts him in the game. We see it in the drive of an academic who is never satisfied with anything less than an A+. We see it playing out in the workplace, in politics, even in our recreation. From the sandbox to the boardroom, the naked desire for stewardship and promotion define who we are. However, this drive is healthy only in the framework of God's intended kingdom purpose. Much like sex in marriage, God created boundaries for our native drive to be used righteously. God told Joshua he would exalt, promote and advance him so the people will know God's presence is with him!

Made for Promotion

This is not the only time God had done this. Consider the life of Joseph.

> *⁴ So Joseph found favor in his sight and attended him, and he made him overseer of his house and put him in charge of all that he had. ⁵ From the time that he made him overseer in his house and over all that he had the Lord blessed the Egyptian's house for Joseph's sake; the blessing of the Lord was on all that he had, in house and field.*
>
> Gen 39:4-5

Joseph was sold out by his brothers, then brought to prominence in the house of an Egyptian official, and finally delivered from jail to the court of Pharaoh where God promoted him to save his family and the future nation of Israel. In like manner, we see Daniel taken into slavery but ultimately favored and promoted for the purposes of God.

> *⁴⁶Then King Nebuchadnezzar fell on his face, worshiped Daniel, and commanded that a grain offering and incense be offered to him. ⁴⁷The king said to Daniel, "Truly, your God is God of gods and Lord of kings and a revealer of mysteries, for you have been able to reveal this mystery!" ⁴⁸Then the king promoted Daniel, gave him many great gifts, and made him ruler over the whole province of Babylon and chief prefect over all the wise men of Babylon.*
>
> Daniel 2:46–48 (NRSV)

As stirring as these stories are, however, they also contain a difficult concept to grasp. Many times, it is temporary demotion that leads to lasting promotion! Indeed, the setback we perceive in our understanding is often the advancement of God leading to the next great thing.

Consider Moses, the greatest leader in the history of Israel. Trained in the finest courts of Egypt, he found himself estranged from his family and hiding in the desert, tending the sheep of his father-in-law. Many times, we find ourselves in demotion or delay, but there are good reasons for it. Perhaps our pride has tied God's hand from acting. *"God opposes the proud, but gives grace to the humble"* (James 4:6). Often, it's our core values which need to be reexamined. Personally, I've learned far more from failure than success. Through demotion, God can work out a necessary humility that releases grace—a grace to be cleansed, healed and transformed so the hand of God can operate in my life.

Whether it was through Moses, Joseph, Daniel or the apostle Paul, we see that God's pathway to promotion can look opposite of man's idea of advancement. I've seen demotion in ministry a number of times, but it proved to be promotion in the Kingdom!

Once, while serving with a major ministry, I had a falling out with the leadership, resulting in a verbal scourging that left a blood trail as I crawled away! To make matters worse, my wife and I were to lead worship for a pastor's conference in 30 minutes. Looking back, I had every right to check out, walk off and resign. I was angry, confused, shaken and hurt. It was more than a demotion, it was a demolition—one that would have changed the course of my life had I given in to the negativity raging within me. Instead, I went ahead with the service. Robie, who was not in the meeting with the leadership, knew immediately that something bad had happened, because my countenance was pale and shaken. But I made a decision to lead worship, to continue to serve and trust

Made for Promotion

God, and to work the situation out later. I understood this to be a testing, and although I perceived it as a demotion, it led to promotion because of my humble response. Today as a lead pastor, as I encounter fire, criticism and other attacks that frequently come with the territory, I realize God used that very situation to prepare me for what lay ahead as he advanced me. The wounding became a blessing—a testing and a qualifier of sorts!

Tragically, when people in church experience valid injury from criticism and slights, they end up pushing the eject button. They become the "done's" of the church, unwittingly running from the very demotion that may be qualifying them for promotion. I know an amazing pastor of a large church who would, in his words, "cross" people as his leaders. He deliberately stressed them to test their response before he would fully set them into positions of responsibility. Sound mean? God certainly tested his men! God tested Abraham, the prophets, and even allowed his own son to be tested!

I recall another test when God asked us to move from a beautiful place with beautiful people and a church we loved, to another place I'd never even heard of. It felt like Jacob being in love with Rachel while her father, Laban, insisted he marry Leah first! It felt like a demotion to me! It was the most difficult thing I have ever walked through. I actually fell on my face in the process and asked God to change His mind or take me home. *Beam me up, Scotty! There's nothing of interest on this hostile planet!*

Still, we obeyed, and I learned some important things in following God through that season.

1) God will lead us in diverse ways. When we moved from a support ministry in eastern Washington to the mountains of

Central Idaho to begin leading a church, there was great joy. We knew God was calling us into a great adventure; it felt wonderful!

2) Sometimes God leads us like the father who just tells us: *"This needs to be done. Go do it."* That is exactly how it felt in a second move we made from Central Idaho to the mountains of North Idaho. Yet in both moves, obedience was the expectation regardless of how he led us! The move felt like a demotion but was actually a promotion! It was truly a matter of optics—all in how you looked at it. In hindsight, I see that God connected us in so many more ways than was possible in our previous location. God allowed the footprint of ministry to be expanded far and beyond what we could have asked or imagined! The move blessed us personally, opened doors of ministry for our family, and strategically rooted us where God knew a fruitful season lay ahead.

Earlier I referenced Isaac, Rachel and Leah. That story is an incredible illustration for how we view ministry in the church. There are areas that seem to be glamorous or "Rachel-like," and others like "Leah," the patient worker. The Bible says that Leah had "tired-eyes" and Jacob was tricked into marrying her first, although Rachel's beauty had captured his heart. Ultimately in that culture, the ability to have children was paramount, and Leah graced Jacob with many more sons than Rachel. I've seen the same in the church body today. Many people aspire to preach on Sundays, lead worship on the platform or serve in some glamorous place when, in fact, they can be much more fruitful serving in humbler surroundings and circumstances. Many times in the promotion of God, those Leah's were actually Rachel's in disguise.

As a pastor and leader, I've also seen things go the other way. Sometimes a man's idea of promotion ends up being a spiritual demotion! I've seen men in a stable spiritual community become lured by promotion and leave for a place where the business climate and educational opportunities are greater. Unfortunately, because these things are elevated on the ladder of their hearts, the move ends up being destructive.

Now, does that mean things such as the economy, the business climate, and other opportunities should never be pursued? Of course not. Factors such as these should be pursued as long as they line up with the mandate of God's Kingdom to influence and ultimately rule in every aspect of life! This is why we must ensure that our priorities are in order, because sometimes the promotion of a man can be a demotion if it removes him from a healthy spiritual community. Any move should fulfill the purposes of God for his family and himself.

God still desires to promote his loving presence in the lives of his people and to set us up for the purposes that lie ahead. We may be flipping burgers at a fast food restaurant or struggling with our educational pathway, but being wholehearted in serving God and consecrating ourselves sets us up for promotion! And when we receive that advancement, let us remember to give God the credit and be sensitive to His desire to further His Kingdom through our lives!

Questions to Ponder:

- What promotions or advances have I seen in the past?
- Have I let past demotions keep me from moving forward?
- Did I recognize God in these demotions?
- Am I ready for more?

Wholehearted - The Crossing

17

Willing Power

> ¹³ *And it shall come to pass, as soon as the soles of the feet of the priests who bear the ark of the Lord, the Lord of all the earth, shall rest in the waters of the Jordan, that the waters of the Jordan shall be cut off, the waters that come down from upstream, and they shall stand as a heap."*
>
> Joshua 3:13 (NKJV)

Like most young boys, I loved bikes. One of the most glorious days of my childhood was when the training wheels came off and I rode on two wheels for the first time. I had arrived! My friends and I used to ride for hours on sidewalks, parking lots and dirt trails. We dressed up those bikes by hanging stuff off the handlebars and clipping playing cards against the spokes to make motorcycle sounds. It worked great until the cards wore out. Of course, our love for all things two-wheel led to dirt bikes. Although my family could not afford one, I had plenty of friends who let me ride theirs.

Later in life, after being married for a couple of years, I purchased my first road bike, the biggest, baddest, fastest thing

Wholehearted - The Crossing

I'd ever been on. It was probably the providence of God that I survived it, to be honest. Still, I learned a valuable spiritual lesson that has served me well to this day. I had been riding for several months when I finally convinced my wife to accompany me. I felt I had enough experience to take her out on the road. So there she was perched behind me with a helmet on. I think I heard "Born To Be Wild" playing somewhere in the distance. It was a great day! Big bad motorcyclist with trophy wife in tow, right? Along the journey, we found ourselves in a situation where the car in front of us was crawling far below the speed limit, so I pulled out to pass. Suddenly, a car pulled out from a driveway and started toward us as we were passing. I had no choice but to crack the throttle to power around the slow vehicle and get back in our lane. Here is the deal—I had NO idea where the power band was on this bike, In fact, I didn't realize there even was a power band! But I quickly found out as the motorcycle exploded with acceleration, propelling us out of danger at speeds far exceeding my expectations. My heart was pounding. So was my head, but that was from Robie smacking my helmet in protest! When my adrenaline finally slowed, I felt foolish. I'd been cruising along on that bike for months, thinking I had it mastered, and it took a *critical situation* for me to find the power band. It was akin to driving a four-cylinder car and having someone sneak a monster Hemi motor under the hood.

Listen: There is a power band in your walk with God that is accessible. Often, we cruise through life never realizing it is available! And yet, Jesus told us that from our innermost being will flow rivers of living water (John 7:30). Water in the natural has the capacity to change everything it touches. Water turns desert landscapes into rich agricultural development. People love living near water. That's why waterfront property is so expensive.

Willing Power

Let's go back to Joshua and learn a valuable lesson about power. In Joshua 3:13, as the people moved toward crossing the river, there two critical components in play.

First, there was a *stated* willingness of God to move in power, making a way through the river of crossing that seemed impossible in the natural. That was the heart of God toward the nation of Israel! Story after story, we read of the power of God displayed for the sake of his people. God moved miraculously in the lives of Abraham, Noah, Moses, Elijah and later, Elisha, who followed Elijah and did twice the miracles. The original disciples experienced the power of God as people were healed and delivered. Narratives abound of people worshipping God in jail and chains falling off. These stories should be more than just memories and Sunday school lectures sharing the bookshelf with fairy tales. They should serve as reminders today that the character of God, his attributes and power, are still the available to us today. There is a power band in our lives if only we would tap it.

Secondly, we see that the crossing did not happen until the priests bearing the ark of the Lord took the first steps into the water. These men carried the presence of God on their shoulders, and in so doing, caused a dynamic reshaping of natural events that enabled Israel to keep moving forward into the promise before them.

Why should it be any different today? I submit that it is not. God is still willing to display his power, majesty and miracles through the lives of those who carry his spirit. With the Spirit of God within us, we bear the responsibility to change the atmosphere wherever we go. However, we need to take the first steps just as the priests did—steps of faith, courage and obedience! Many times, we are just cruising through life unaware of the power band available, forgetting that it takes a first step for us to move into it. It can be a prompting in our spirit or the sudden appearance of an oncoming car that causes us to experience the dynamic power shift. The truth is that we were created to be the recipient of the willing power of God in our lives. It's not what God wants to do *to* us, but *through* us!

Notice in our opening scripture that the priests stepped into the water at the beginning of crossing over. This is powerful prophetic imagery. Jesus talked about "living water," which is a promised resource for believers.

> *"But whoever drinks of the water that I will give him shall never thirst; but the water that I will give him will become in him a well of water springing up to eternal life."*
>
> John 4:14

> *[37] Now on the last day, the great day of the feast, Jesus stood and cried out, saying, "If anyone is thirsty, let him come to Me and drink. [38] He who believes in Me, as the Scripture said, 'From his innermost being will flow rivers of living water.' "*
>
> John 7:37-38

Throughout the New Testament, Jesus talked about water, walked on water, promised water and used water for the foundation of his first miracle!

> *[6] Now there were six stone waterpots set there for the Jewish custom of purification, containing twenty or thirty gallons each. [7] Jesus said to them, "Fill the*

waterpots with water." *So they filled them up to the brim.*

John 2:6-7

We know the pots were stone and thus ceremonial because clay pots were considered impure for ceremonial purposes. Hence, Jesus took something filled only enough to be ceremonial and filled it full to be useful.

It is also worth noting that the number six in the Bible represents the number of man. So when I read this story, I wonder if we are full enough with the Holy Spirit—the Water of the Word—or are we only deep enough in the River of Life to be ceremonial?

Water in the natural is a precious resource. A few years ago, I was ministering in the San Joaquin Valley where I encountered many signs that read: *"War On Water."* One of the locals explained that the agriculture in that valley supplied close to seventy percent of our nation's produce. Now however, because of an endangered fish, as well as the demands of the rest of the state of California, there was a competition for water. This contention has been labeled the *War On Water*. Let's look at an account of another *War On Water* in the Old Testament.

> *[12] Now Isaac sowed in that land and reaped in the same year a hundredfold. And the Lord blessed him, [13] and the man became rich, and continued to grow richer until he became very wealthy; [14] for he had possessions of flocks and herds and a great household, so that the Philistines envied him. [15] Now all the wells which his father's servants had dug in the days of Abraham his father, the Philistines stopped up by filling them with earth.*

Wholehearted - The Crossing

Genesis 26:12-22

The Philistines were similar to the enemy we face today, one that is envious of God's provision for believers and his willingness to display his power. In Issac's day, it was a tactic of war to take a city, fill the wells and stop the flow of water.

Today, spiritual wells face annihilation. How many of us have said, at one time or another, "I feel dry?" Without living water, we become ceremonial at best. We may look the part but we lack enough substance to be useful. As such, we fail as the foundation of the miraculous that God desires to pour through us.

> *[16] Then Abimelech said to Isaac, "Go away from us, for you are too powerful for us." [17] And Isaac departed from there and camped in the valley of Gerar, and settled there. [18] Then Isaac dug again the wells of water which had been dug in the days of his father Abraham, for the Philistines had stopped them up after the death of Abraham; and he gave them the same names which his father had given them.*

Genesis 26:16-18

The story of Isaac re-digging of the wells of his father teaches us an important lesson. We cannot live on the wells of our ancestors, our friends, or even our pastor! Yes, we can be refreshed in those wells, but how will we sustain ourselves or be the refreshing for someone else?

> *[19]But when Isaac's servants dug in the valley and found there a well of spring water, [20]the herdsmen of Gerar quarreled with Isaac's herdsmen, saying, "The water is ours." So he called the name of the well Esek, because they <u>contended</u> with him. [21]Then they dug*

> *another well, and they <u>quarreled</u> over that also, so he called its name Sitnah.*
>
> Genesis 26:19–21 (ESV)

There are many things the enemy uses to stop up the supply of living water in our lives.

CONTENTION

As stated earlier, an ancient tactic of the enemy was to use stones and dirt to destroy wells. The enemy we have today uses spiritual means. Contention will stop the flow of the water Jesus declared for us. It is interesting that prophetically, Isaac named the well *Esek,* which in Hebrew means contention. Now, there is a contention for the faith that Paul writes about in Jude 3, but contention between believers is a sure way to hinder the flow of the Holy Spirit in our lives.

To gage the contention among us, we should ask whether we are known more for what we believe in or what we are against. It is too easy to slip into "protest Christianity" and become the people who are contentious rather than those who build bridges of relationship leading to sharing the gospel with our neighbors. I understand there are non-negotiable issues worth contending for, but these should be vastly outnumbered by our overwhelming positive positions on issues, starting with the love of God.

I suspect David had a few contentious thoughts as he was about to encounter Goliath. David journeyed from the back forty, where he tended his father's sheep, to the frontline of the battle bearing supplies. He got in a lot of trouble for asking a simple question.

> *"What will be done for the man who kills this Philistine and takes away the reproach from Israel?*

> *For who is this uncircumcised Philistine, that he should taunt the armies of the living God?"*
>
> 1 Samuel 17:26

> *²⁸Now Eliab his oldest brother heard when he spoke to the men; and Eliab's anger burned against David and he said, "Why have you come down? And with whom have you left those few sheep in the wilderness? I know your insolence and the wickedness of your heart; for you have come down in order to see the battle." ²⁹But David said, "What have I done now? Was it not just a question?" ³⁰Then he turned away from him to another and said the same thing; and the people answered the same thing as before.*
>
> 1 Samuel 17:28-30

What strikes me about this encounter is that David saw the big picture even as a lesser conflict tried to interfere, forcing David to choose which "hill to die on." He could have argued with his brother Eliab, but ultimately there were no spoils to winning that battle. Instead, David turned from Eliab, moved on and would not take the bait!

To be honest, our nature as believers in Christ can be contentious. We will fight to be right even when there is nothing to win save the empty satisfaction of our perceived victory. It's no wonder the Christian church is known more for what it's against than what it is for! Now there is certainly room for "iron sharpens iron," and the examination of sound doctrine is necessary. But that's not what I'm talking about. The apostle Paul says it best:

> *Nor to pay attention to myths and endless genealogies, which give rise to mere speculation rather than*

Willing Power

> *furthering the administration of God which is by faith.*
>
> 1 Timothy 1:4

Paul was addressing early church dynamics that still apply today. We, as a believing people, spend an inordinate amount of time contending about non-consequential things! We are "dying on hills" that have no spoils, ultimately stopping the wells that God wants flowing from our lives.

Early in the development of the music ministry, I remember churches contending against drums being set up under the cross hanging on the front wall. I also recall discussions of whether a bass guitar belonged in a church or a bar! There have been contentions about worship styles, carpet color, banners, which Bible translations should be used—the NIV (Nearly Inspired Version), the ESV (Everybody's Saved Version) or the venerable KJV to please the King James Only crowd.

Earlier, I explained that my experience as a road musician playing rock and roll ended with my salvation. As I understood my commitment to Christ, I made a decision to sanctify (or "set apart") my music for God's purpose. My wife and I had been attending our local church for a couple of years when I was finally invited to play my electric guitar for the worship service. I was nervous but excited as my love and passion for music was allowed to express my love for Christ. I'd finally been taken off the leash! At the end of the service—I remember to this day—the oldest lady in the church slowly made her way toward me carrying her ten-pound Bible. I knew what was coming—the great church smack down about playing "that electric guitar." She walked up to me, looked me straight in the eye, pointed her crooked finger at me and said, "Sonny, you just keep playing that electric guitar in church!" I was free!

For too long, believers have been distracted by contentions, going to war over trivial issues with no spoils to win!

QUARRELING

Take another look at Isaac digging a well and notice that he called the second well *Sitnah*, which means "quarreling," a cousin of contention

> ²¹ *Then they dug another well, and they quarreled over that also, so he called its name Sitnah.*
>
> Genesis 26:19–21 (ESV)

The Bible has plenty to say in regards to *Sitnah*, but the overriding theme is that quarreling stops wells.

> *It is better to live in a corner of the housetop than in a house shared with a quarrelsome wife.*
>
> Proverbs 21:9 (ESV)

> *It is better to live in a desert land than with a quarrelsome and fretful woman.*
>
> Proverbs 21:19 (ESV)

> *As charcoal to hot embers and wood to fire, so is a quarrelsome man for kindling strife.*
>
> Proverbs 26:21 (ESV)

> *...not a drunkard, not violent but gentle, not quarrelsome, not a lover of money.*
>
> 1 Timothy 3:3 (ESV)

> *And the Lord's servant must not be quarrelsome but*

Willing Power

kind to everyone, able to teach, patiently enduring evil,

2 Timothy 2:24 (ESV)

Nowhere does the Bible say anything good about quarreling, instead calling it sin. It even disqualifies a person from leadership in the church. Yet in our culture, we have turned it into an art form! It is easier to fall into arguments than agreement. From the talking heads on television to social media bickering, we certainly see more contentious quarreling than we do agreement. We do well to heed God's word: *"How good and pleasant it is when brethren dwell together in unity, for there will God command a blessing"* (Psalm 133:1).

The Bible also speaks of submission when it tells us to be subject on to another and wives submit to their husbands (ref. Ephesians 5:21-22). We even have the admonition to *"Obey your leaders and submit to them, for they keep watch over your souls as those who will give an account* (Hebrews 13:7). Note, however, that submission is only needed where there is no unity. And, when true contention is needed, it should be to contend for unity so that the wellsprings of life will flow!

I learned an important principle from a great leader, Bill Graybill, on how to be a peacemaker. There is a critical difference between a problem and a tension. Knowing each is crucial in bringing peace and unity in tough circumstances. A problem is something you solve; a tension is something you manage. The tensions of life will always be with you! To know the difference, we must ask: Is this a problem to be solved or a tension requiring constant management? For example, in family life, there are problems and there are tensions. Teenagers, for example, are not necessarily problems, but they present a variety of tensions as they grow and mature. (Yeah, I'm a man of faith.)

In the constant building of living stones into a spiritual house, there will always be tensions to walk through. However, when we confuse these with problems to be solved, we become easily entangled in contentious and quarrelsome things that plug the wells of living water.

Of course, these are not the only things the enemy uses to stop our wells! We see that offenses, bitterness, gossip, misdirected priorities, materialism and certainly sin destroy those wells! We cannot continue to live in sinful ways and expect the resources of the Kingdom of God to flow like rivers in our lives!

The man lying by the pool of Bethesda is an illustration of this.

He was 38 years in his sickness when Jesus healed him. The man received God's work, took up his pallet and began to walk. End of story? Not hardly.

> *Afterward Jesus found him in the temple and said to him, "See, you are well! Sin no more, that nothing worse may happen to you."*
>
> John 5:14 (ESV)

I'm not sure what the man's sins were but it's hard to imagine being sick for 38 years, not strong enough to put yourself in the pool. Obviously, he was an invalid. What worse could happen? I suspect the worse condition was spiritual. Jesus was telling him that sin stops up the wells of living water! During his 38 years, the man was sick but had not given up hope. Going back to a sinful lifestyle—perhaps one he had before he got sick—would have eliminated all vestiges of God's power in his life.

Willing Power

In healing the man by the pool of Bethesda, Jesus changed ceremonial waters into living waters that healed. The world's culture that God intends us to affect will not be changed by ceremonial Christianity which holds *"to a form of godliness, although they have denied its power"* (2 Timothy 3:5).

Just as Joshua and those with him were poised to step into the water, cross over and forever change what was on the other side, we have the same opportunity and, I submit…responsibility! Yet it will only happen when we find the power band of our spiritual resources and understand that there is "willing power" available from God. There is a vast difference between ceremonial water and living water! We are promised living water. It's needed, it's essential and it's available!

> *[Issac] moved away from there and dug another well, and they did not quarrel over it; so he named it Rehoboth, for he said, "At last the Lord has made room for us, and we will be fruitful in the land."*
>
> Genesis 26:22

The Lord has made room for us—a room for the purposes, dreams and blessings lying before us. As we are called to be fruitful in this journey of life, so we need the living water of God.

Questions to Ponder:

- Is the Holy Spirit present in my life?
- What could be stopping the flow of this incredible power in my life?
- Is it time for me to step into the water?

Wholehearted - The Crossing

18

Available Men

> ¹*Now Moses was pasturing the flock of Jethro his father-in-law, the priest of Midian; and he led the flock to the west side of the wilderness and came to Horeb, the mountain of God.* ² *The angel of the Lord appeared to him in a blazing fire from the midst of a bush; and he looked, and behold, the bush was burning with fire, yet the bush was not consumed.* ³*So Moses said, "I must turn aside now and see this marvelous sight, why the bush is not burned up."*
>
> Exodus 3:1-3

The incredible truth of Christianity is that God has designed us for relationship with him. The reciprocal of this truth is that our lives will not be fulfilled without the release of his plans and purposes working through our lives. We see this in the story of Moses and his interaction with God.

This story is well know. Moses tried and failed to deliver Israel and was now a goat herder tending the flocks of his father-in-law. What a fall from a palace prince to the desert goat herder! All because there were things in God's heart to be accomplished.

And I say to you that there are still things in God's heart to be accomplished!

> The Lord said, "I have surely seen the affliction of My people who are in Egypt, and have given heed to their cry because of their taskmasters, for I am aware of their sufferings.
>
> Exodus 3:7

God conditioned Moses for forty years, but now it was time to move on behalf of his people Israel, starting with an incredible discourse.

> Moses said to God, "Who am I, that I should go to Pharaoh, and that I should bring the sons of Israel out of Egypt?"
>
> Exodus 3:11

Not an auspicious start, eh? Moses was having an identity crisis, which is not uncommon for leaders thrust into a new challenge. Speaking directly to the issue, God answered Moses' question of "Who am I?"

> [12]He said, "Certainly I will be with you, and this shall be the sign to you that it is I who have sent you: when you have brought the people out of Egypt, you shall worship God at this mountain." [13]Then Moses said to God, "Behold, I am going to the sons of Israel, and I will say to them, 'The God of your fathers has sent me to you.' Now they may say to me, 'What is His name?' What shall I say to them?" [14] God said to Moses, "I AM WHO I AM"; and He said, "Thus you shall say to the sons of Israel, 'I AM has sent me to you.'
>
> Exodus 3:12-14

Available Men

Here is the incredible part. In the midst of Moses' identity crisis, God demonstrated that he was going to be with Moses, positioning himself through Moses to enable this great deliverance. But Moses still had questions and objections!

> Then Moses said, "What if they will not believe me or listen to what I say? For they may say, 'The Lord has not appeared to you.'"
>
> Exodus 4:1

Now, I suspect Moses was still on fairly good ground with God. The problem was that Moses knew he did not have what it took to carry out the purposes of God in himself. In return, God's answers demonstrated that he is willing to supply what was needed. Let this example give us greater confidence as well as we move ahead!

> ² The Lord said to [Moses], "What is that in your hand?" And he said, "A staff." ³ Then He said, "Throw it on the ground." So he threw it on the ground, and it became a serpent; and Moses fled from it. ⁴ But the Lord said to Moses, "Stretch out your hand and grasp it by its tail"—so he stretched out his hand and caught it, and it became a staff in his hand— ⁵ "that they may believe that the Lord, the God of their fathers, the God of Abraham, the God of Isaac, and the God of Jacob, has appeared to you." ⁶ The Lord furthermore said to him, "Now put your hand into your bosom." So he put his hand into his bosom, and when he took it out, behold, his hand was leprous like snow. ⁷ Then He said, "Put your hand into your bosom again." So he put his hand into his bosom again, and when he took it out of his bosom, behold, it was restored like the rest of his flesh.
>
> Exodus 4:2-7

Despite the encouragement of these miraculous signs, however, the insecurity of Moses rose up again. The patience of God here amazes me. What would our response be not only to the burning bush, but to the promise of God that further signs and wonders would be at our disposal? Yet Moses moved to doubt his ability as a spokesman, and God overcame his final objection.

> [10] Then Moses said to the Lord, "Please, Lord, I have never been eloquent, neither recently nor in time past, nor since You have spoken to Your servant; for I am slow of speech and slow of tongue." [11] The Lord said to him, "Who has made man's mouth? Or who makes him mute or deaf, or seeing or blind? Is it not I, the Lord? [12] "Now then go, and I, even I, will be with your mouth, and teach you what you are to say."

This should have been the end of the conversation, or at least the end of Moses! But Moses had one last thing to say to the Almighty.

> [13] But he said, "Please, Lord, now send the message by whomever You will."

> [14] Then the anger of the Lord burned against Moses, and He said, "Is there not your brother Aaron the Levite? I know that he speaks fluently. And moreover, behold, he is coming out to meet you; when he sees you, he will be glad in his heart.

Exodus 4:13-14

Notice what made God angry. It was not Moses' past failures, deficiencies or insecurity, nor his lack of giftedness or ability! No, God did not disqualify Moses for his past; in fact, he promised to make Moses strong.

Available Men

Moses presented the ONLY attitude that made God angry!

Moses told God he was UNAVAILABLE!

Un-avail-ability.

Many people have ability, but without the "avail" part, they are useless! And it can anger God! Even though God is willing to display His power through us, it's our insecurity or lack of faith that causes us to make ourselves unavailable.

For example, consider the following from a church bulletin.

> Our church was saddened to learn this week of the death of one of our most valued members, Someone Else. Someone's passing creates a vacancy that will be difficult to fill. Else had been with us for many years, and for every one of those years, Someone did far more than a normal person's share of the work. Whenever there was a job to do, a class to teach, or a meeting to attend, one name was on everyone's list, "Let Someone Else do it." Whenever leadership was mentioned, this wonderful person was looked to for inspiration as well as results; "Someone Else can work with that group." It was common knowledge that Someone Else was among the most liberal givers in our church. Whenever there was a financial need, everyone just assumed Someone Else would make up the difference. Someone Else was a wonderful person; sometimes appearing superhuman. Were the truth known, everybody expected too much of Someone Else. Now that Someone Else is gone, we wonder what we are going to do.

Rather than our *abilities*, it's our lack of *availability* that is the greatest hindrance to God. As Christians, we walk with a God who has purpose, dreams and plans to restore broken people. Therefore, the desire of God to move through us is not for our benefit or exultation, but in response to his heart for the broken people around us. Paul writes to a young leader in Timothy;

> *The things which you have heard from me in the presence of many witnesses, entrust these to faithful men who will be able to teach others also.*
>
> 2 Timothy 2:2

God is looking for F.A.T. people: Faithful people who are Able to Teach. In a word: *AVAILABLE*. We don't want people wandering for years in the wilderness because of our being unavailable! No matter what situation you are in, moving forward have faith that God is willing!

Questions to Ponder:

- Have I heard God call me aside for his purpose?
- Have I ever been unavailable for God?
- How can I become available?

19

Making Memories

⁴ Then Joshua called the twelve men whom he had appointed from the children of Israel, one man from every tribe; ⁵ and Joshua said to them: "Cross over before the ark of the Lord your God into the midst of the Jordan, and each one of you take up a stone on his shoulder, according to the number of the tribes of the children of Israel, ⁶ that this may be a sign among you when your children ask in time to come, saying, 'What do these stones mean to you?'

Joshua 4:4-6 (NKJV)

On the journey of our lives, many memories are made. Some great, some OK, and honestly, some we would like to forget. In this media-driven age, it's easy to share our memories worldwide; some apps even remind us to re-share memories from a few years past. While we can't live in the past, the memories of God's work in our lives can be encouragement for those around us—a testimony to the next generation. In crossing over, it's interesting that Joshua called men specifically to build a memorial for the coming generations. Indeed, there is a responsibility to answer the inevitable questions as they study what God and men have done in the name of God…with stones.

Stones have always garnered fascination in history. What would we do without them? Whether historical markers, walls, castles, graves, inscribed or not, stones have a place of significance. An early sixteenth-century church I visited once in Chittingstone England, had the original church fathers buried under the floor. The headstones bearing their names were in the stone flooring we walked on. Talk about walking over dead bodies to experience new life! Gave new meaning to "founding fathers."

Stones have been used to mark memories, as tools for agriculture, and also tools of execution. From the Rolling Stones to "Everybody Must Get Stoned," stones have found a place in the lexicon of modern life. In college, a Christian friend of mine got the opportunity to address the secular student body. His famous opening line? *"Most of you have something in common with the Apostle Paul, like you, he was stoned a number of times!"*

In Exodus 20, God wrote the Ten Commandments on two stones that Moses delivered to the people. Kinda hard to argue with something engraved in stone.

In Genesis, Jacob and Laban used stones as part of a covenant.

> [43] *Then Laban replied to Jacob, "The daughters are my daughters, and the children are my children, and the flocks are my flocks, and all that you see is mine. But what can I do this day to these my daughters or to their children whom they have borne?* [44]*"So now come, let us make a covenant, you and I, and let it be a witness between you and me."* [45]*Then Jacob took a stone and set it up as a pillar.* [46]*Jacob said to his*

Making Memories

> kinsmen, "Gather stones." So they took stones and made a heap, and they ate there by the heap. [47]Now Laban called it Jegar-sahadutha, but Jacob called it Galeed. [48]Laban said, "This heap is a witness between you and me this day." Therefore it was named Galeed,
>
> Genesis 31:43–48

In Joshua 24, we see that Joshua did the same for a covenant at Shechem.

> [25]So Joshua made a covenant with the people that day, and made for them a statute and an ordinance in Shechem. [26]And Joshua wrote these words in the book of the law of God; and he took a large stone and set it up there under the oak that was by the sanctuary of the Lord. [27]Joshua said to all the people, "Behold, this stone shall be for a witness against us, for it has heard all the words of the Lord which He spoke to us; thus it shall be for a witness against you, so that you do not deny your God."
>
> Joshua 24:25–27

Speaking of the stone, Joshua said that "it has heard all the words spoken." That might sound weird, but it reminds me of Jesus' admonition that if his people were kept from praising him "*the stones will cry out!*" (Luke 19:40).

Obviously, it took men of strength and courage to build stone memorials. Consider one stone per man, hauled over great distances; these were not pebbles. It also took courage. Joshua's men were asked to go back across the Jordan River to do this. Keep in mind this was the river in which the waters were parted…but for how long?

There are good memories for sure, but some of the most impactful memories are of struggles we have walked through in life. America's Memorial Day commemorates the fallen soldiers who served our country. The Bible has an account in 1 Samuel regarding the victory over the enemy of Israel.

> [11]*The men of Israel went out of Mizpah and pursued the Philistines, and struck them down as far as below Beth-car.* [12]*Then Samuel took a stone and set it between Mizpah and Shen, and named it Ebenezer, saying, "Thus far the Lord has helped us."* [13]*So the Philistines were subdued and they did not come anymore within the border of Israel. And the hand of the Lord was against the Philistines all the days of Samuel.*
>
> 1 Samuel 7:11–13

The stone was even named! *"Thus far the Lord has helped us."* The symbolic nature and physical presence of that stone reminded the Philistines as well: Don't mess with God's people!

In Genesis, Abraham built altars of remembrance to God everywhere he went. Every time God blessed him, he started building! (Do you think he had a building committee?)

Joshua understood the significance of memorial stones as a remembrance of covenant and deliverance. I'm not certain he envisioned what God would eventually build with stones—the new temple as the spiritual house of the living church, but he was certainly on the vanguard of its formation.

> [4]*And coming to Him as to a living stone which has been rejected by men, but is choice and precious in*

Making Memories

the sight of God, ⁵you also, as living stones, are being built up as a spiritual house for a holy priesthood, to offer up spiritual sacrifices acceptable to God through Jesus Christ.

1 Peter 2:4–5

God uses living stones, but certainly not perfect stones. Yet it is our irregularities that allow us to mesh with other imperfect stones, relying on the Chief Cornerstone, Jesus. It is here that memories are being made.

God is intent on making memories of our lives. The steps of our consecrated journey are the living stones that further God's kingdom. I want my life to have significant memories along the way—not memories to live in the past, but memories like the stones of old that remind, encourage, and spur future generations to move on in Kingdom life.

How about you?

Questions to Ponder

- What memories have been created through my life?
- What "God" memories have been created?
- What does it mean to me to be a "living stone"?

Wholehearted - The Crossing

20

The Why of the Wilderness

> [2]*And you shall remember that the Lord your God led you all the way these forty years in the wilderness, to humble you and test you, to know what was in your heart, whether you would keep His commandments or not.* [3]*So He humbled you, allowed you to hunger, and fed you with manna which you did not know nor did your fathers know, that He might make you know that man shall not live by bread alone; but man lives by every word that proceeds from the mouth of the Lord.*
>
> Deuteronomy 8:2–3 (NKJV)

The wilderness has always captured my heart. From classic movies like *Jeremiah Johnson* to modern tales like *The Revenant*, (about the true-life frontiersman and trapper Hugh Glass), I'm enthralled by wilderness tales. I've had plenty of experiences, from horseback hunts up into the Pasayten Wilderness in the mountains of Washington State, to exploring the expanse of the John Day Wilderness area, and delving into the edge of the Frank Church River of No Return Wilderness. The sheer breathtaking beauty of

God's creation, including encounters with bear—no, I did not kill it with a knife—bugling elk and rutting moose, are all tucked away in the notebook of my mind.

The wilderness is full of sounds. The strangest I've ever heard was a primordial grunt in the bass frequency, both guttural and ethereal. Upon careful exploration, I discovered it belonged to a bull moose on a quest for company of the opposite moose-sex. Fortunately, I did not fit the bull (bill?).

The smells in the wilderness are also unique—dark, damp earth scents mingled with pine, fir and cedar trees. The animals also leave unique scents. Elk have a sweet aroma that lingers long after they pass. And moose? The smell will assault your senses. It's the worst of all odors in my book (and this *is* my book, after all).

While the great outdoors invokes a sense of romance, it can also be harsh and unforgiving. People get lost, caught unprepared, and often pay for it with their lives.

Taken together, however, these elements impart a wonder of the wilderness.

In the story of Israel's wilderness excursion, we often brush by what God accomplished through it. Their experience was more than merely the just consequences of faithlessness. Enduring the wilderness speaks of becoming fit, physically and spiritually, being prepared to move forward.

The wilderness of the Sinai desert does not fit any experience I've had. It is barren, harsh and hostile. There is no rainfall and little vegetation. The only water is from the occasional oasis, enough to survive but not thrive. And yet this is the experience God used to condition his people.

The Why of the Wilderness

Why?

Wilderness experiences humble us. The children of Israel had to learn to completely trust God for their survival.

It's the same today. In all my years exploring wilderness areas, I never lost my way. Then I was invited to bow hunt for elk in the John Day Wilderness area of Oregon. It was a crisp fall morning the day we arrived. After setting up camp, I decided to venture forth alone on an afternoon hunt. I found a promising game trail which led me into some prime elk habitat. I was enraptured exploring this new area. A couple hours later, I realized I was a fair bit from my camp and needed to start back. An hour later, it dawned on me that I was turned around somehow and had lost my way. I hiked up a mountain only to climb back down searching for a landmark. I tried to find my way again and again, all to no avail. I was working hard and drenched with sweat—not good with a cold fall evening approaching—and completely out of water as well. I felt fear creeping in with the encroaching darkness. Foolishly, I had left camp unprepared for an overnight stay, eschewing the prime directive of any survival training.

At this elevation, I knew the danger of hypothermia was real. I pushed myself harder and to my relief, I came upon someone's uninhabited spike camp. There was a tent, a large container of water and the other camp trappings, but no one around. *Should I stay and hope someone would come in? Should I just get some water and continue trying to find my way back?* It was dusk; I was cold, wet and needing to make a decision. *Start a fire in the camp? Climb into the tent and sleeping bag?* Awkward at best and certainly humbling.

Earlier I talked about sounds in the wilderness. Here is where that came into play. As my thoughts raced and my prayers grew desperate, I heard a distant ringing. I couldn't be sure where it was coming from or if I was imagining it. In a few minutes, my rescuer rode into camp on horseback accompanied by a dog wearing a bell! For being lost, I could not have found a better campsite. It belonged to a Mennonite group. They soon returned from the day's treks and helped me get dry and warm. They fed me, broke out guitars, and pointed me in the right direction. I found my own camp before nightfall and slid into my own sleeping bag grateful for the lesson on God's providence over self-reliance. Getting lost now seemed like a blessing.

One of God's purposes for the wilderness experience was to humble Israel. I'm not sure why they needed to be humbled. They'd been in captivity for hundreds of years, slaves with no identity, despised and abused. Yet they needed to be humbled.

It's the same with us. Pride creeps in, self-reliance is bred by short-sighted success, and we began believing our own press, much of which is self-authored! Pride interferes with the grace God wants to pour into our lives, so in his love for us, he deals with it.

> *But he gives more grace. Therefore it says, "God opposes the proud but gives grace to the humble."*
>
> James 4:6 (ESV)

Humility is the gateway to receive God's grace. I have felt the opposition of God and realized the trigger is almost always pride. There are a few instances of positive pride or confidence we read in Paul's letters to the church. However, there is a tipping point when it becomes inflated and egotistical. Pride was the downfall of Kings Uzziah and Hezekiah, as well as Herod. Pride not only affects individuals, but can bring down nations.

The Why of the Wilderness

Haughty eyes and a proud heart, the lamp of the wicked, are sin.

Proverbs 21:4 (ESV)

[16]There are six things that the Lord hates, seven that are an abomination to him: [17]haughty eyes, a lying tongue, and hands that shed innocent blood,

Proverbs 6:16–17 (ESV)

Pride is impossible to internalize. It effects not only our thoughts and attitude, but is evidenced in our speech, our looks, even our body language. We see it manifest in how we judge others. Once again, I'm not sure why Israel needed to be humbled in the wilderness, but pride can creep in subtly. And when it does, there is a principle of opposition that comes from God.

In our lives, there is an incredible need for grace. We need grace personally and for others as well. The most incredible and blessed people are those whose lives exhibit the grace of God pouring through the gates of humility.

I've had a number of wilderness experiences in my life. They have taught me to seek God's purposes for the experiences. One might be to always prepare for the worst when following a promising elk trail. How about you?

Questions to Ponder:
- What wilderness experiences have I walked through?
- Do I struggle with pride?
- Can I identify where the grace of God has been released to me?

Wholehearted - The Crossing

21

The Heart in the Wilderness

> *"In the wilderness He fed you manna which your fathers did not know, that He might humble you and that He might test you, to do good for you in the end."*
>
> Deuteronomy 8:16

The wilderness was to not only humble the people of Israel, but to test their hearts. We find out who we are in times of failure. There is a testing of life that comes and goes—mostly *comes* I think—and reveals what has been elevated to priority on the ladder of our hearts.

Biblically, the heart is known as the center of man's will, the place of decision. It can be startling how deceptive we can be... even to ourselves. The wilderness is used by God to reveal us and redeem us. There is no doubt what we are made of when faced with our own annihilation. Even though Joshua and Caleb were commended for being wholehearted, I believe there was a continuing development for them as well in the wilderness!

We are all on a journey to cross over, an unfinished walk with plenty of promise ahead. I have found that many times in considering my own maturity, which is the goal of a believer, that a consistent level of testing is required for our lives to maintain a Kingdom priority. King David was man after God's own heart but he also wrote, *"Search me oh God, and know my heart"* (Psalm 139:23). David invited the testing! That took more courage than facing a bear, a lion, or even Goliath!

Let's consider the heart. In the beginning, man was created perfect, good and with wholeness of heart. With the introduction of sin, however, there was an erosion of that heart, affecting the seat of our will, thinking and decisions. Now, through Jesus, we see the promise of a new heart as recorded in Ezekiel.

> *And I will give them one heart, and a new spirit I will put within them. I will remove the heart of stone from their flesh and give them a heart of flesh,*
>
> Ezekiel 11:19 (ESV)
>
> *And I will give you a new heart, and a new spirit I will put within you. And I will remove the heart of stone from your flesh and give you a heart of flesh.*
>
> Ezekiel 36:26 (ESV)

We also see many New Testament passages identifying decisions and responsibilities we have in regards to our newly redeemed hearts.

James 4:8 tells us to *"purify your hearts..."*

Hebrews 3:8 speaks of not *"hardening your hearts..."*

Romans 10:9-10 says to *"believe in your heart...."*

Ephesians 4:32 encourages us to *"be kind to one another, tenderhearted..."*

1 Peter 3:15 admonishes us: *"but in your hearts, honor God..."*

The Heart in the Wilderness

There is an incredible story in the life of David concerning Mephibosheth that illustrates the heart of God. David was finally established as the new king of Israel and there was peace in the kingdom. When a new king would arrive, however, he would remove and destroy the heirs of the previous king. Yet David's heart was different; it was like God's.

> *Then David said, "Is there yet anyone left of the house of Saul, that I may show him kindness for Jonathan's sake?" ² Now there was a servant of the house of Saul whose name was Ziba, and they called him to David; and the king said to him, "Are you Ziba?" And he said, "I am your servant." ³ The king said, "Is there not yet anyone of the house of Saul to whom I may show the kindness of God?" And Ziba said to the king, "There is still a son of Jonathan who is crippled in both feet."*
>
> 2 Samuel 9:1-3

We first hear about Mephibosheth in 2 Samuel 4:

> *Jonathan, Saul's son, had a son who was lame in his feet. He was five years old when the news about Saul and Jonathan came from Jezreel; and his nurse took him up and fled. And it happened, as she made haste to flee, that he fell and became lame. His name was Mephibosheth.*
>
> 2 Samuel 4:NKJV

In the story, the nurse fled from the new king, not knowing David's heart toward them. In that flight, the nurse fell and Mephibosheth was injured and crippled for life. We see most of the time that biblical names point to a person's character and destiny. Mephibosheth's name meant "an exterminator of idols."

The nurse's fear of David, however, caused him to be removed from his destiny and purpose!

I have seen people run away from the King because they don't know His heart to bless them, to love them, provide for them and heal them. In the process of fleeing, most become hurt and distanced from their destiny. Yet if they only knew God's heart, they would run *to* him instead of *away* from him!

> *⁶ Mephibosheth, the son of Jonathan the son of Saul, came to David and fell on his face and prostrated himself. And David said, "Mephibosheth." And he said, "Here is your servant!" ⁷ David said to him, "Do not fear, for I will surely show kindness to you for the sake of your father Jonathan, and will restore to you all the land of your grandfather Saul; and you shall eat at my table regularly." ⁸ Again he prostrated himself and said, "What is your servant, that you should regard a dead dog like me?" ⁹ Then the king called Saul's servant Ziba and said to him, "All that belonged to Saul and to all his house I have given to your master's grandson. ¹⁰ You and your sons and your servants shall cultivate the land for him, and you shall bring in the produce so that your master's grandson may have food; nevertheless Mephibosheth your master's grandson shall eat at my table regularly."*
>
> 2 Samuel 9:6-10 (NKJV)

Note that Mephibosheth's fear was not only that he was Saul's grandson, but also that he was lame. Culturally there was a bias against the lame and the blind even in David's heart because of the past. Let's look at another passage in the Bible.

The Heart in the Wilderness

> *⁶ Now the king and his men went to Jerusalem against the Jebusites, the inhabitants of the land, and they said to David, "You shall not come in here, but the blind and lame will turn you away"; thinking, "David cannot enter here." ⁷ Nevertheless, David captured the stronghold of Zion, that is the city of David. ⁸ David said on that day, "Whoever would strike the Jebusites, let him reach the lame and the blind, who are hated by David's soul, through the water tunnel." Therefore they say, "The blind or the lame shall not come into the house."*
>
> 2 Samuel 5:6-8

There would seem to be a bias in David's heart earlier on in response to the mocking of his enemies. Also, in the culture, the priest could not enter the Holy of Holies if he had an imperfection, such as lameness, blindness or many other *"blemishes."*

> *"The Hebrews say there are in all 120 blemishes which disable the priest-eight in the head, two in the neck, nine in the ears, five in the brows, seven in the eyelids, nineteen in the eyes, nine in the nose, nine in the mouth three in the belly, three in the back, seven in the hands, sixteen in the secrets, eight in any part of the body, eight in the skin, and seven in the strength and in the breath.*
>
> *****
>
> *Formerly, the Church of England was very cautious in admitting to her ministry those who had gross personal defects, but now we find the hump-backed, the jolt-headed, bandy-legged, club-footed, one-eyed,*

etc., priests even of her high places. Why do our prelates ordain such?

(from Adam Clarke's Commentary, Electronic Database. Copyright (c) 1996 by Biblesoft)

We even see that when Jesus was about to heal a blind man, he was asked a question that revealed a cultural bias.

> *² And his disciples asked him, "Rabbi, who sinned, this man or his parents, that he was born blind?" ³ Jesus answered, "It was not that this man sinned, or his parents, but that the works of God might be displayed in him."*
>
> John 9:2–3 (ESV)

So Mepibosheth had a lot stacked against him. Not only was he Saul's grandson but he was also physically imperfect, a dead dog! But God loves lame people! He wants to cover them, to heal them and restore them. We know that David shared God's heart on the matter because he allowed Mepibosheth to live and prosper.

The following story from Matthew illustrates the heart of God towards people, including us!

> *³⁰ Then great multitudes came to Him, having with them the lame, blind, mute, maimed, and many others; and they laid them down at Jesus' feet, and He healed them. ³¹ So the multitude marveled when they saw the mute speaking, the maimed made whole, the lame walking, and the blind seeing; and they glorified the God of Israel.*
>
> Matthew 15:30-31 (NKJV)

The Heart in the Wilderness

As we consider Mephibosheth, it's clear that he chose to focus on his lameness despite hearing the heart of David the king. Still, Mephibosheth was invited to sit at the king's table much the same way we have been invited to partake of communion—the table of the Lord. Interestingly, as he sat at the table, he was unable to see his lame feet because of the king's invitation.

If we fully understood the heart of God towards us, we would not run away but would run to him! We would stop focusing on our lameness, or other people's lameness, and understand that God intends to heal and restore us. God's provision covers our lameness! That is the heart of God illustrated through David, the same heart God wants to renew in you and me!

When I consider the lives of Joshua and Caleb, I see that a personal determination was made in their journey with God—a determination that, joined with God's design from the beginning of creation and a deliberate act of their will, was to serve God fully as "wholehearted." We see the results, are inspired and challenged by them.

It takes courage to be wholehearted. As I've stated from the beginning, it also takes a decision and a firm step on our part. Just as sin crept into the heart of Adam, neither are we are immune to its effects. Yet because of the heart of God, we can be restored to the pathway. Many times, it takes a testing, humbling and submission before God to shape us into His image.

> *The wilderness served many purposes for Israel, one of which was to test their hearts. Personally I do not care for the chastening of the Lord, but I know that it is done out of love and for the purpose I've asked. To fully serve, to be a wholehearted man, for the Lord*

reproves him whom he loves, as a father the son in whom he delights.

Proverbs 3:12 (ESV)

For the Lord disciplines the one he loves, and chastises every son whom he receives."

Hebrews 12:6 (ESV)

Questions to Ponder

- What have wilderness experiences revealed about my heart?
- Do I have the courage to ask God to "know my heart"?
- Do I recognize that I am truly a son or daughter?

22

Wilderness Strong

Then Joshua rose early in the morning; and he and all the sons of Israel set out from Shittim and came to the Jordan, and they lodged there before they crossed. 2 At the end of three days the officers went through the midst of the camp; 3 and they commanded the people, saying, "When you see the ark of the covenant of the Lord your God with the Levitical priests carrying it, then you shall set out from your place and go after it.

Joshua 3: 1- 3

Joshua describes the picture of Israel's preparation as, *"after three days the officers went through the camp."* It takes preparation to move from old things into new things. Consider the fitness required of Israel to make the crossing, engage the opposition and ultimately gain what God had desired.

Our nation is obsessed with exercise and nutrition. We know we ought to do better. Sometimes we try, experience a season of success, only to collapse into greater failure. We see the result of fitness; we want it but we won't work for it.

I recall a humorous story years ago, written by a woman

struggling to get into shape.

> *Determined to lose weight, I decided to join a fitness class that met three times a week. But no matter how much I pleaded, my husband, Keith, refused to join me. As the weeks went by, my excuses for missing most of the classes became more and more creative. On the morning of playing hooky from yet another exercise class, Keith said, "Honey, if I'd known you were going to miss so many classes, I would have joined with you."*

We instinctively love strength, how it looks and feels. Any phrase with "strong" attached is deemed positive. We have "battle-strong," "Army-strong," even a fitness program designed around throwing bales of hay, lifting tractor tires, and cleaning barns: "farm-strong."

The wilderness experience in Sinai was God's design to produce a spiritually fit and healthy Israel—to make them wilderness strong! Without spiritual fitness, we cannot move forward in our crossing!

That is what the wilderness was designed to do! It is the process of God working in our life, bringing us to a spiritually fit and healthy place that enables us to move forward. Mark Batterson wrote: *"It took a day for God to take Israel out of Egypt, but forty years to get Egypt out of Israel."*

Yes, under harsh conditions we can rebel against God's desires and be swayed by bad influences, but ultimately we will grow to survive. Israel had seen miraculous deliverance, plagues brought down on Egypt, and had endured an unforgiving climate through the provision of God. In turn, God used the wilderness to sift the people, sorting the weak from the strong, the committed from the cravenly fearful, and ended up with a people who were spiritually fit and ready to move into a new season.

So how are you preparing yourself? The task in front of you dictates the preparation.

I prepare differently depending on the challenge—playing music, hunting, fly fishing or being trounced in basketball by some kid half my age. Recently, the fall bowhunting season for elk was before me, and even though I try to stay in some semblance of shape year round, I knew the sheer physicality of hiking up and down mountains would be much more than I was prepared to give. So I start adding distance, weights and bike riding to my exercise routine. I told Robie recently that in my mind, I am still thirty, but my fifty-five year-old legs don't lie!

So how do we prepare to be spiritually fit? Well, just as physical exercise strengthens the heart, spiritual exercise strengthens the heart of believers. And while physical fitness relieves overall stress on the body by raising our metabolism and enabling us to remain active, so spiritual fitness does the same for our inner man. It gets rid of excess flab, changes our motivation, improves our self-esteem, and eliminates a host of ailments common to the lackadaisical and sedentary. Spiritual strength is an amazing counter-force for addictions, bad habits, gloomy paradigms, anxiety, cynicism, and a critical spirit that sucks the life out of us.

Here's an indictment of a critical spirit in influencing bad spiritual health.

> *Do not speak evil of one another, brethren. He who speaks evil of a brother and judges his brother, speaks evil of the law and judges the law. But if you judge the*

law, you are not a doer of the law but a judge.

James 4:11 (NKJV)

So, what are the exercises of a disciplined life that lead us to physical and spiritual strength?

First of all, natural fitness is a combination of disciplines that combine physical exercise and healthful eating habits. A few years back, I decided that I needed more accountability when it came to my physical well-being. I had a lot of dreams ahead of me and did not want my body to limit what was in my heart. So I hired a personal trainer for a few sessions to give me a fitness test and frame up an exercise routine. It was more comprehensive than I expected, however, as he targeted different muscle groups, core strengths and so on. Of course, I didn't get in shape instantly, but I had the blueprint for the discipline to bring it to pass!

Discipline! I don't know of too many people who love discipline. When you become a believer and your language begins to change—you know those old familiar cuss words? It seems they get replaced by other words like *discipline!* Joking here, of course, but the reality of life is that it takes discipline to accomplish anything worthwhile. Being a *disciple* without *discipline* just doesn't work.

Recently I've read a devotional by Mark Batterson entitled *Chase the Lion*. One of the chapters deals with stewarding the things of purpose that God drops into our hearts and imaginations. Mark writes that we make these things obedient to Christ via blood, sweat and tears. He states: *"If your dream is a book, you make it obedient with a keyboard. If your dream is playing professional sport, you make it obedient at the gym. If your dream is making music, you make it obedient one note at a time."*

Wilderness Strong

One of God's purposes for the wilderness was to develop in the children of Israel a lifestyle of worship.

Spiritual fitness is achieved by developing a lifestyle of worship through a combination of disciplines. To many, worship is about the song service part of a church liturgy and nothing more. But true worship involves the positioning of the heart, not unlike positioning the body at a gym. We gain spiritual strength by assuming positions of humility, adoration and Godly focus.

A lifestyle of worship requires developing an intimate time of relationship in our journey with God. When Moses led Israel out of Egypt, it took a day for them to escape and eighteen months for them to learn worship.

> *And He said, "Certainly I will be with you, and this shall be the sign to you that it is I who have sent you: when you have brought the people out of Egypt, you shall worship God at this mountain."*
>
> Exodus 3:12

We all need private worship with the Lord; it is a necessity for the blessing and the strength that comes from it. Think of family and relationships. Certainly, there should be always a time of gathering, eating, sharing and making memories. Robie and I value these times, but for our relationship to be healthy and balanced, we also require *private time*—our own time to focus on what is near and dear to our hearts. If the only time I spent with Robie was in a crowd, it would be unhealthy.

Most outdoorsmen have a secret place we like to visit, a place of tranquility that we are reluctant to share with anyone, even those closest to us. I even know guys who are protective of where they get firewood! Secret places are where we have found success—the best fishing, hunting, meditation, painting, photography or just saying "Ahhhh...."

I spent a few days hunting with a friend, during which we shared a small camp trailer. I soon realized my daily routine of grabbing a cup of joe and having some alone-time with the Lord was a bit cramped. I ended up just pulling my hoodie over my head and shutting out everything to focus on God. I don't do well without my private time. Things don't work as easily, my thoughts don't align as well, I'm not as nice of a person. Honestly, my wife needs me to have "that place," my neighbor needs me to have "that place", my dogs need me to have "that place"…of private time with God! (The Elk? Not so much.)

Finding my secret place has been instrumental in my growth as a follower of Christ. King David speaks of finding that place and the benefits of it.

> [1]*He who dwells in the secret place of the Most High shall abide under the shadow of the Almighty. [2]I will say of the Lord, "He is my refuge and my fortress; my God, in Him I will trust." [3]Surely He shall deliver you from the snare of the fowler and from the perilous pestilence. [4]He shall cover you with His feathers, and under His wings you shall take refuge; His truth shall be your shield and buckler.*
>
> Psalm 91:1–4 (NKJV)

The word *"dwells"* speaks of "sitting down, remaining and abiding." It is a deliberate act of our will. The secret place refers to a private time of personal worship and prayer with the Lord.

The two main excuses most people give for not praying is that they don't have time and they don't have a place to go. Susanna

Wilderness Strong

Wesley, who was the mother of John and Charles Wesley in the 1700s, had 19 children. If anybody had an excuse for not praying, it was her. Yet Susanna spent an hour in prayer every day. So where does a mother of 19 go to escape? Nowhere! She took her apron and flipped it up over her head and spent an hour in prayer every day. Her children knew to not disturb her in that time because mother was in her apron praying.

As a pastor, I know that if I could influence everyone to develop a personal time of devotion, worship & prayer, it would absolutely impact each family, workplace and community. Nothing around us would be the same.

In my secret place, God encourages me about my identity in him. He deals with my insecurities, my frustrations, speaks to me about my sin and the forgiveness that is afforded. He gives me wisdom, strength and direction for each day. I receive divine interaction that sustains me through the struggles of life. I can speak to him about my dreams and defeats; he speaks to me about new dreams and alignments that are needed for my life.

Here are some key things that happen when you are in that secret place:

First of all, you develop an authentic relationship with God through an added element of intimacy. Experiencing the corporate presence of people is different than the private presence; it's the same with God. They are both necessary to build relationships.

There is an intimacy and empowering with God that he wants to happen, and it certainly impacts who you are and what you become! Moses knew that secret place.

> *So the Lord spoke to Moses face to face, as a man speaks to his friend. And he would return to the*

> camp, but his servant Joshua the son of Nun, a young man, did not depart from the tabernacle.
>
> Exodus 33:11 (NKJV)

> So it was, whenever Moses went out to the tabernacle, that all the people rose, and each man stood at his tent door and watched Moses until he had gone into the tabernacle.
>
> Exodus 33:8 (NKJV)

We don't develop the kind of intimacy and relationship that we were created for simply by watching God, or watching others interact with God.

> But since then there has not arisen in Israel a prophet like Moses, whom the Lord knew face to face,
>
> Deuteronomy 34:10 (NKJV)

> [16] Nevertheless when one turns to the Lord, the veil is taken away. [17] Now the Lord is the Spirit; and where the Spirit of the Lord is, there is liberty. [18] But we all, with unveiled face, beholding as in a mirror the glory of the Lord, are being transformed into the same image from glory to glory, just as by the Spirit of the Lord.
>
> 2 Corinthians 3:16–18 (NKJV)

Secondly, a secret place is a place that leads to success and reward, as the following passage describes.

> He who dwells in the secret place of the Most High
> Shall abide under the shadow of the Almighty.
>
> Psalm 91:1–4 (NKJV)

Wilderness Strong

In Matthew 6:4 (NIV), Jesus said, *"your father who sees in secret will himself reward you openly."* It speaks of charitable deeds and rewards, but also states that God sees us in secret!

Thirdly, we begin to practice God's presence in our secret place! Disciplines that we have committed to are practiced. Let me elaborate. We must practice inviting God into our lives, spending time with him, talking with him in prayer. There is literally nothing on the earth you can be good at without some sort of practicing! From a study on great people and their achievements, I learned that it takes 10,000 hours to obtain mastery in any field. As an example, Tiger Woods was ranked number one for 13 years, during which time he hit more than 1000 golf balls a day. That's 4 million golf balls!

God wants to talk with you, hear your voice, and listen to your thoughts. There are a million distractions comprising the noise of our culture intent on drowning out the voice of God. Finding a consistent secret place of worship, prayer, and God's Word will be the most important step you make in your lifestyle of worship as a believer.

Make the decision, invest the time, and find a secret place!

Wholehearted - The Crossing

23

Stronger Together

Not forsaking our own assembling together, as is the habit of some, but encouraging one another; and all the more as you see the day drawing near.

Hebrews 10: 25

When God spoke to Moses concerning the people worshipping him on the mountain, he was addressing their need to learn how to come together corporately. Under the oppression of slavery, they had little opportunity to exercise their faith. As part of their deliverance, God was intent on restoring the spiritual fitness of the people, starting with a lifestyle of worship.

Balance is necessary in all aspects of life. Athletes know there are numerous disciplines and skills needed, not just the ones visible to viewers. A basketball player, for example, can't just be a shooter. A golfer can't just be a putter. Successful people master balance.

This is why God has given us a myriad of expressions of worship. As such, we cannot worship God solely in our own way. In Genesis, we see that Cain desired to worship God in his own way and not as prescribed by God. Unfortunately, it was disaster for him personally, and also for his wife (whoever she was).

This is why the corporate gathering of God's people keeps us healthy. It fulfills the purpose of teaching us the ways in which God desired to be worshiped. Although we call it "going to church," it is certainly much more than just attending a community meeting of believers. Being planted, committed and serving in a church is biblical and certainly God's will for his people. It is there that we are equipped, strengthened and purposefully fit together, making us spiritually stronger than we could ever be on our own. Yes, we *are* the church, but there is an assembly that God requires.

A number of years ago, my wife and I had the opportunity to build our own home. After years of renting and even buying a couple of fixer-uppers, the door opened for us to have a contractor build our dream home from the ground up.

So we purchased a small piece of property, inked the contract with the builder, and often drove by to check on progress. One day the foundation was being carved out of the earth, ready for forms and fittings. A week later the concrete was set. On one of our visits, there was a huge delivery of lumber on the property—laminated beams, trusses, studs and nails. It was our house but it wasn't our house.

Somewhere in those bundles of deforested wilderness, our house lay before us but it wasn't our house until it was assembled! Despite the plans, the dreams and the financing, it took *assembling* to make it a reality! We called it our house, but it wasn't fulfilling its purpose because it had not been put together! In the ensuing months, the blueprints which had been burned into our imaginations became a real product. The dream finally became reality.

It's the same for the church. The dream in the heart of God for

Stronger Together

building Jesus' church to manifest his glory on the earth requires an assembling of the chief components—us!

My oldest son taught us a thing or two about this. He was fresh out of high school and waiting for Bible college to begin, so he went to work for a local construction company. Now, McCall, Idaho, is a small resort community in the mountains of central Idaho. Sixty percent of the homes are second homes for wealthy people. Many are custom designed houses costing a million dollars or more. I was home one day when Drew asked if I would take a ride with him so I could see some of the houses he had helped build. We would drive by a home and he would point out the beams, decks or entryways that he had built. I felt his pride of accomplishment, and was blessed that he wanted to share what he had built. Then it dawned on me that there is a spiritual parallel at work as well. Just as my son was building something and wanted to share it with his father, Jesus is also building a house—the church that bears his name—and it is for the glory of *his* father! Amazing! We are privileged to be included in the forming, the fitting, the purpose and the glory that is being built. The Bible says the latter house will be even greater in glory than the former house! It's not drudgery, habit or religious duty for me and my family to be planted in a church family; it's being part of the house where the Glory of God abides!

Actually, the story of our custom built house has another side to it.

In answering the call of God for vocational ministry as a lead pastor, I had resigned from a wonderful company and begun leading a small congregation. For the first three years, our family lived in an aged parsonage the church provided. It was older than dirt. We had to burn six cords of wood a year to keep it warm, and we prayed the wind would not blow the rusted metal roof off! After a time, we felt divine inspiration to buy a home of our own, set down some roots and start to bloom. After looking at numerous houses and not finding anything that fit our family, our realtor directed us to meet with a Christian contractor about possibly building something for us. That had never entered our thinking, as the cost was above our pay grade for sure! Yet the man we met had a dream for building a pastor a home at *his* cost. Incredible! He explained how we could do it. Throughout his years of building, there was always left-over and imperfect lumber, siding, beams, roofing material and such. If we were willing to work with imperfect materials, he could put many of these components together for our custom home. We agreed and he set to work.

The framers commented on the rough and twisted lumber, but in the hands of a master builder, the home was incredible. And it was ours! In fact, several years later when God called us to serve in another place, that home sold for three times what we had put into it, with two parties actually bidding higher than our asking price in the midst of a huge drop in the real estate market! That house, built with B-grade lumber and cast offs, was fashioned into a quality, custom home much greater in value when assembled by a master craftsman.

It reminds me of King David gathering with four hundred men in the cave of Abdullam. The story described those men as indebted, depressed and discouraged, and yet they gathered together to serve the purpose of God under the authority of a king. In time, these B-grade individuals were assembled together and became known as David's mighty men. So much like our lives!

Stronger Together

> *⁴As you come to him, a living stone rejected by men but in the sight of God chosen and precious, ⁵you yourselves like living stones are being built up as a spiritual house, to be a holy priesthood, to offer spiritual sacrifices acceptable to God through Jesus Christ.*
>
> 1 Peter 2:4–5 (ESV)

Peter is referring to us as living stones built together into an incredible house that Jesus will proudly display. Remarkably, he is not using perfect stones! God calls the misshapen, the odd, the abused, the cast off and leftovers. Yes, we fit into his house, but some assembly is required. In that work of God, we move from the glorious blueprint in the heart of Jesus to the reality assembled into a house that he can present to his father!

We see a picture of God's church in the O.T. Nehemiah…

> *⁵Ezra opened the book in the sight of all the people for he was standing above all the people; and when he opened it, all the people stood up. ⁶Then Ezra blessed the Lord the great God. And all the people answered, "Amen, Amen!" while lifting up their hands; then they bowed low and worshiped the Lord with their faces to the ground.*
>
> Nehemiah 8:5–6

We see also an imperative verse in the New Testament!

> *…not forsaking our own assembling together, as is the habit of some, but encouraging one another; and all the more as you see the day drawing near.*
>
> Hebrews 10:25

It's interesting to discover what people think about a gathering of believers. You can learn a lot by their response to certain words. Mention "church," and you may hear: *religious, boring, legalistic, political, out of date, not needed, hurtful, overbearing, useless*. And while some of this can be true at times, their reaction is also evidence of the warfare being waged against the gathering and assembling of God's people.

Even church-going people have various reasons for coming to church.

- Maybe it's a drug problem—mom *drug* them to church every Sunday.
- Maybe it's for the social aspects—seeking a girlfriend or spouse.
- Maybe it's out of habit, such as an ex-nun.
- Maybe it's to set an example for our kids.
- Maybe it's to set an example for our parents.
- Maybe we come out of desperation or despair.
- Maybe we're seeking to strengthen our marriages.
- Maybe we have children who have strayed, and we're hoping a different environment will give us the tools to help them.

Fundamentally, God's design was that in all aspects of relationship and worship, the corporate gathering *would be part of that expression.*

In the early church, being part of a committed local body was an essential component of their service and worship. Acts 2:46 states, "*So continuing daily with one accord in the temple,*

Stronger Together

and breaking bread from house to house, they ate their food with gladness and simplicity of heart." It was a vibrant community with a commitment to gathering.

In addition to fellowship, we see that there is a different sense and dimension of God's presence in the corporate gathering that is designed to be part of our lifestyle of worship. Take the example of a phone call, text or a personal encounter. There is an element of connection and presence in each one of these modes of communication, but the dimension of each is totally different!

In the Old Testament, God dwelt in the midst of his people by way of the tent of meeting (the tabernacle), and the priests encountered God there on behalf of the people.

> *And let them make me a sanctuary, that I may dwell in their midst.*
>
> Exodus 25:8 (ESV)

In the New Testament we find something different.

> *[4] As you come to him, a living stone rejected by men but in the sight of God chosen and precious, [5] you yourselves like living stones are being built up as a spiritual house, to be a holy priesthood, to offer spiritual sacrifices acceptable to God through Jesus Christ.*
>
> 1 Peter 2:4–5 (ESV)

Just as we can experience a unique relationship with God privately in our secret place, so we can also experience a powerful dimension of God's presence in the corporate gathering of God's people. Indeed, most lives are impacted through the corporate gathering, especially in the early stages of Christian growth.

Wholehearted - The Crossing

In the Old Testament, the Chief Priest entered the Tabernacle and encountered the presence of God resting there. In the New Testament, however, a different pattern emerged.

> *[19]So then you are no longer strangers and aliens, but you are fellow citizens with the saints, and are of God's household, [20]having been built on the foundation of the apostles and prophets, Christ Jesus Himself being the corner stone, [21]in whom the whole building, being fitted together, is growing into a holy temple in the Lord, [22]in whom you also are being built together into a dwelling of God in the Spirit.*
>
> Ephesians 2:19-22

In the Old Testament, God's presence rested in the tabernacle, but in the New Testament, the Bible says we are a *"nation of priests and kings."* Today, God's presence rests in an incredible dimension in and on his people!

Let me state this again! The presence of God rests on the gathering of God's people as they come together. The individual is a key part of the whole picture! This is way beyond a mere personal relationship with the Almighty.

Here are some keys when considering the assembling of ourselves together.

First, we must realize that it is a high calling.

David, a man after God's own heart, couldn't wait to go to church!

> *I was glad when they said to me, "Let us go to the house of the Lord!*
>
> Psalm 122:1 (ESV)

Stronger Together

Jesus, after being tempted and tested, began his ministry by going to church!

> And He came to Nazareth, where He had been brought up; and as was His custom, He entered the synagogue on the Sabbath, and stood up to read.

Secondly, we must have the right focus.

Often, we come to church focused on ourselves or others. While this sounds noble, it is not in the right order. Remember that the priest in the Old Testament first focused on ministering to God, and then on ministering to people. In that respect, we are called to operate as the priests did.

> But you are a chosen race, a royal priesthood, a holy nation, a people for his own possession, that you may proclaim the excellencies of him who called you out of darkness into his marvelous light.
>
> 1 Peter 2:9 (ESV)

We gather together to give and not to get! Let us come together to serve God first and serve God's people second. If you come to get, you will ultimately be disappointed. God does not respond to a consumer mentality. Being only a spectator will eventually turn you into a critic. If you don't believe that, just wait until you are watching the NFL and you inevitably turn into an armchair quarterback!

Recall our earlier discussion of sanctification: It literally means "to set apart" for special use or purpose, to make holy or sacred. In Joshua 3:5, the people are told, *"sanctify yourselves."* Sanctification, therefore, involves a deliberate act of our will. It involves our time, talent and treasure, and as such, it becomes holy unto the Lord.

Wholehearted - The Crossing

When we sanctify ourselves in gathering with other believers, it is a holy time. As we come together as worshipers and givers, we sanctify the assembly and ultimately leave fulfilled. Pastor Mark Patterson describes the church gathering as providing "sanctuary light."

In the Old Testament, the shekinah glory of God rested in the temple just beyond the curtain. Today, the presence of God rests on his people as they gather together and experience the glory of God. His glory changes us, shifts our paradigms, and reveals God's perspective. Walking solely alone can make us weird, out of balance, susceptible to strange theology from self-proclaiming wilderness prophets, or some guy on a computer still living in his mom's basement blasting out religious spam to the unsuspecting masses while being accountable to no one.

God sees things through a redemptive lens. Without his presence, we tend to see through a lens of bitterness, unforgiveness, discouragement and death-centered theology.

Asaph was one of the three worship leaders who rotated in tabernacle service under David's leadership. Twelve of the songs in the book of Psalms have been attributed to him. Apparently he fell off the rotation for a while because in the beginning of Psalm 73, we read his negative, critical and pessimistic view of life. In verse 16, Asaph not only had issues with understanding, but was deeply troubled as well. Then starting in verse 17, something changed. He came into the sanctuary of God and encountered God's presence!

> *1 Surely God is good to Israel, to those who are pure in heart! 2 But as for me, my feet came close to stumbling, my steps had almost slipped. 3 For I was envious of the arrogant as I saw the prosperity of the wicked.*
>
> Psalm 73:1-3

Stronger Together

¹⁶ When I pondered to understand this, it was troublesome in my sight ¹⁷ until I came into the sanctuary of God; then I perceived their end.

Psalm 73:16–17

The glory of God resting corporately on his people changes how they view things! Our Godly perspective is restored and our understanding deepens. The world has a way of superimposing its image upon us. In the assembling of God's people, we acquire our Kingdom perspective!

Recall from Nehemiah that when the people gathered to worship and celebrate, it says the *"the joy of the Lord is our strength"* (Nehemiah 8:10). In the corporate gathering, our strength is recovered as God works through us to encourage, edify and exhort one another. Gathering and committing to the house of God keeps us balanced and accountable as we build one another up into a holy temple. The Bible promises that the glory of the last house will be greater than the former. In the presence of God there is incredible transformation as his glory rests on his people.

Yes, our lives are impacted by finding that secret place of personal relationship. Yet we cannot neglect the gathering of his people, or being planted as a part of his church. Corporately, we pray together, weep together, sharpen one another, comfort one another, minister together, grow together, and become what Jesus is building—his church.

The church is not perfect; it's full of people. But it's being perfected through the glory of God resting on her. It rests on all of us as we come together to minister, serve the Lord, and then serve on another.

> *¹² The righteous man will flourish like the palm tree, he will grow like a cedar in Lebanon. ¹³ Planted in the house of the Lord, they will flourish in the courts of our God. ¹⁴ They will still yield fruit in old age; They shall be full of sap and very green, ¹⁵ To declare that the Lord is upright; He is my rock, and there is no unrighteousness in Him.*
>
> Psalm 92:12-15

God used the wilderness to sift, strengthen and ultimately drive Israel to a place of spiritual fitness where they became strong and sound. God prepared them as a nation to cross the Jordan river into the Promised Land, ready and able to face whatever challenges lay before them!

God wants you to be fit, to have courage, to be "God strong." As you move into the new, can you take a moment to assess where you are spiritually?

Before us lie the promises of God born of the dreams and imaginations of our Creator's heart. With these come challenges, strongholds, and battles, requiring us to be spiritually fit as we advance.

Questions to Ponder:

- What keeps me from being planted in a community of believers?
- Have I faced my hurts, bitterness, and disappointments as possible reason for my isolation?
- Is it time to break my isolation habit and join the gathering?

24

The Marking

> *¹ So it was, when all the kings of the Amorites who were on the west side of the Jordan, and all the kings of the Canaanites who were by the sea, heard that the Lord had dried up the waters of the Jordan from before the children of Israel until we had crossed over, that their heart melted; and there was no spirit in them any longer because of the children of Israel. ² At that time the Lord said to Joshua, "Make flint knives for yourself, and circumcise the sons of Israel again the second time." ³So Joshua made flint knives for himself, and circumcised the sons of Israel at the hill of the foreskins.*
>
> Joshua 5:1-3 (NKJV)

Striding through the forest on a photo shoot, bow hunt or nature hike, we see marks everywhere. A rutting whitetail buck rubs his antlers on tree bark, leaving an unmistakable sign of his presence. An amorous moose destroys a bush, announcing to his rivals that he means business. A bear rips up a decayed stump, dislodges a boulder, or defecates prominently against a tree as a sign of territorial supremacy.

In like manner, we dwellers in the wilderness of modern society leave our marks. We append our signatures to agreements, tattoo our skin, and wear shirts bearing the insignias of our favorite market branded objects. Throughout existence, there have been markings and those determined to leave their mark on the earth.

God—the father of creation—desires to leave his mark on the lives of men. We see this in the life of Joshua. He led the people over the river into the Promised Land, and God instructed Joshua to mark the men. Circumcision speaks of being marked as different from any other culture. In this case, it was to signify the end of their shame: the shame of an unbelieving generation still infected by Egypt. The history of 400 years of slavery had not only *marked* them with shame, but also *marred* them. Added to this was the continual shame of wandering for forty years in the wilderness after the glorious delivery from Egypt, knowing they had disappointed God. Can you imagine the mocking spirit coming from Egypt about their God rescue resulting in a wilderness banishment until an entire generation died off?

As gross as it sounds today, the hill of the foreskins was important to the newly minted men of Joshua's culture. It was a place of marking where God reminded the people of his covenant with Abraham. It bore tremendous spiritual significance to them in moving forward.

> *And the Lord your God will circumcise your heart and the heart of your descendants, to love the Lord your God with all your heart and with all your soul, that you may live.*
>
> Deuteronomy 30:6 (NKJV)

The Marking

> *For we are the circumcision, who worship God in the Spirit, rejoice in Christ Jesus, and have no confidence in the flesh,*
>
> Philippians 3:3 (NKJV)

> *In Him you were also circumcised with the circumcision made without hands, by putting off the body of the sins of the flesh, by the circumcision of Christ,*
>
> Colossians 2:11 (NKJV)

Rooted in God's directive to mark his people was his desire to set them apart, give them a new heart and new hope, and remove the shame of their bondage. Joshua 5:9 explains this further.

> *Then the Lord said to Joshua, "This day I have rolled away the reproach of Egypt from you." Therefore the name of the place is called Gilgal to this day.*
>
> Joshua 5:9 (NKJV)

Today, God wants to roll away the reproach of our past, erasing the vestiges of our captivity and condemnation, marking us for his own.

From previous chapters, recall my story of being separated from my biological father as a child and not knowing my legal given name. It is interesting what growing up fatherless in the natural can do to a boy. I find that in God's design, there is an imprint or marking that a father makes on the life of a son or a daughter. There is purpose modeled and imparted, an identity assured and reinforced. In my searching as I grew, I experienced an incredible void in these areas. God blessed my mother, but she was never created by God to mark a son like a father can. She could mentor, nurture and educate, but in a different way than a father is designed by God to do. Studies show an astounding percent of youth crime, suicides, homelessness, depression and other social issues are linked to fatherless families. Even the apostle Paul noted that there were many teachers, but not many fathers. Why? I believe that if God designed fathers to mark their children, then the strategy of the enemy is to destroy that relationship just as we see in our culture today. In the natural sense, I was eventually reunited with my father and my given name. Through this encounter, I experienced a sense of identity and belonging I never imagined—a removal of shame and insecurity as I realized that I was family. It was everything I'd always wanted and planned for in the beginning!

In Joshua 5, *Gilgal* means "wheel" or "rolling." God marked the men of Israel as they moved forward, and removed, or "rolled away," the reproach of their captivity in Egypt as a lifestyle they were never created for. It is the same for us today. When we surrender and accept the call of God on our lives through Jesus, there is a supernatural circumcision, a marking if you will, along with a rolling away of reproach from the old way of living.

> *Therefore if anyone is in Christ, he is a new creature; the old things passed away; behold, new things have come.*
>
> 2 Corinthians 5:17

As newly minted Christians, one of the issues we face is moving forward with an enemy who constantly reminds us of our past. This is why we often feel condemnation over stupid things we thought or did in our former, unregenerate state. Children of divorced parents are especially hard hit with this tendency, bearing the notion that they are responsible for the destruction of the home.

The Marking

Fortunately for the redeemed, there is a truth that sets us free.

> *We are destroying speculations and every lofty thing raised up against the knowledge of God, and we are taking every thought captive to the obedience of Christ,*
>
> 2 Corinthians 10:5

This scripture speaks not only of stewarding our thoughts but of the freedom realized through the mark of God on our lives. As Christians, we are his people; God has marked us as his own. He wants to advance, direct, heal and ultimately spend eternity with us.

As we crossover into new things, taking fresh territory, we must realize that God's desire for relationship not only marks us as his own but washes us clean, rolling away the sin, shame and defeats of the past. That does not mean we don't occasionally bear the consequences of sin, but in our failures there comes greater measures of success in our lives.

Questions to Ponder

- How have I been marked by my past, good or bad?
- How has God changed my past?
- How has God marked me for the future?

Wholehearted - The Crossing

25

Overcoming Opposition

Now Jericho was tightly shut because of the sons of Israel; no one went out and no one came in. ² The Lord said to Joshua, "See, I have given Jericho into your hand, with its king and the valiant warriors. ³ You shall march around the city, all the men of war circling the city once. You shall do so for six days. ⁴ Also seven priests shall carry seven trumpets of rams' horns before the ark; then on the seventh day you shall march around the city seven times, and the priests shall blow the trumpets. ⁵ It shall be that when they make a long blast with the ram's horn, and when you hear the sound of the trumpet, all the people shall shout with a great shout; and the wall of the city will fall down flat, and the people will go up every man straight ahead."

Joshua 6:1-5

The stories about Joshua are not only real events, but also a prophetic picture we can apply today. In the passage above, Joshua, Caleb and Co. crossed the river and then faced an obstacle before them that had to be overcome. Jericho was the oldest city of that time, and a strategic opposition that needed to be defeated in order to possess the land. To Israel, it was the gateway to the Promised Land. To us today, Jericho represents the unavoidable challenges in our lives, sometimes requiring wisdom, other times endurance. To the Jews staring at the unassailable walls surrounding this ancient city, however, the unconventional and supernatural power of God was the only thing that could overcome the barrier standing between them and their destiny.

What are the oppositions in your life that prevent you from walking in all that Christ has obtained for you? We all have things we try to go around, ignore, or make disappear, but until we deal with them with God's help, they keep us from the blessing God desires for us. Consider the old saying: "No matter where you go, there you are!" How many times do we break out into a fresh season, throwing off the remnants of the previous challenge while embracing our new lease on life, only to be confronted with yet another barrier, be it physical, financial or relational?

So here are the children of Israel finally crossing over into the inheritance that God had promised, yet facing another obstacle that must be met head on. It didn't help that Jericho knew they were coming.

> *Now Jericho was tightly shut because of the sons of Israel; no one went out and no one came in.*
>
> Joshua 6:1

Israel's presence before the rugged walls, coupled with the testimony that preceeded their arrival, changed the normal flow of life in Jericho. Commerce, industry and travel came to a grinding

Overcoming Opposition

halt. It is an amazing reminder that we can change the places that we walk in. As we face our modern Jericho's, we must remember the atmosphere-changing potential of Christ that is always present as we carry the Spirit of God within us. *"Christ in you, the hope of Glory"* (Colossians 1:27) is a reality. Far from some new religious philosophy devoid of power or influence, it's real, dynamic and yet often taken for granted.

After the death and resurrection of Jesus, his disciples gathered in a closed room, fearing for their lives and uncertain over the future. They'd staked everything on their charismatic leader and now he was gone. Or was he? In John 20:22, we see that Jesus appeared in their midst and *"he breathed on them and said to them, 'Receive the Holy Spirit.'"* Something changed in that moment. Nothing on the outside of those four walls was different, but inside, each disciple experienced the transformative power of God's spirit. Some say the church was established and empowered on the day of Pentecost (Acts 2), but I believe that the inauguration of the church began when Jesus breathed on them behind closed doors. There is an atmosphere-changing potential within each of us because of the presence of the Holy Spirit and commission of Jesus!

God told Joshua he would give him everywhere that the sole of his (Joshua's) feet touched That is an atmosphere-changing promise. Israel's presence standing *outside* Jericho changed normal life *within* Jericho. (Well, it destroyed it. But you don't get more transformative than that.) Similarly, the presence of God in our lives today changes destinies, families and communities by bringing life. Mention being a Christian in any circumstance and you will get a reaction! The report and testimony of our lives brings the power of God to change the places we walk from death to life. So walk well; walk with humility and boldness; walk where change is needed, and change where you walk!

> *The Lord said to Joshua, "See, I have given Jericho into your hand, with its king and the valiant warriors.*
>
> Joshua 6:2

Notice that God had already given Jericho into Joshua's hand. It was in God's mind and so was as good as done. Much like our lives, God is not waiting to see if we do good before deciding our future. He has already purposed and fashioned wonderful things for us, but there are walls that need to come down for us to possess those things. Previously when viewing the Promised Land, the people looked at things the wrong way!

> *"Where can we go up? Our brethren have discouraged our hearts, saying, 'The people are greater and taller than we; the cities are great and fortified up to heaven; moreover we have seen the sons of the Anakim there.'"*
>
> Deut 1:28

This is what can happen when we walk by sight and not by faith. They saw things that caused them to be discouraged. What we see must be combined with faith for the balance to come into our lives. Joshua 6:2 speaks of God seeing the victorious outcome before we do. It's already in the mind of God, waiting for us to walk it out.

> *"You shall march around the city, all the men of war circling the city once. You shall do so for six days."*
>
> Joshua 6:3

There is a constant contrast of competing cultures that influence the way we choose to walk out this life. From the Aerosmith song, *Walk this Way*, to aspiring models being taught

Overcoming Opposition

how to walk, even to a fishing technique called "walking the dog," everywhere you turn there is influence being exerted over how we go through life! The truth is that if you want to overcome life's obstacles, becoming *"more than conquerors"* (Romans 8:37), we must walk in obedience! It is essential to overcoming difficulties and pulling down strongholds! Jericho was just such an obstacle; it was a barrier to blessing, and God gave Israel specific instructions on how to walk.

> *[6] Therefore as you have received Christ Jesus the Lord, so walk in Him, [7] having been firmly rooted and now being built up in Him and established in your faith, just as you were instructed, and overflowing with gratitude.*
>
> Colossians 2:6-7

Biblically speaking, walking in God speaks of behaving! We cannot expect the blessings of God if we walk in opposition to the direction flowing from God's heart. We cannot continue in sin, dismissing it by thinking it does not have an impact on our future. Paul wrote:

> *What shall we say then? Are we to continue in sin so that grace may increase? May it never be! How shall we who died to sin still live in it?*
>
> Romans 6:1-2

We are to walk with endurance as Joshua and the Jews did.

> *[4] "Also seven priests shall carry seven trumpets of rams' horns before the ark; then on the seventh day you shall march around the city seven times, and the priests shall blow the trumpets. [5] "It shall be that when*

> *they make a long blast with the ram's horn, and when you hear the sound of the trumpet, all the people shall shout with a great shout; and the wall of the city will fall down flat, and the people will go up every man straight ahead."*
>
> Joshua 6:4-5

Seven days? I'm OK with once, twice, but can you imagine about the 4th or 5th day? I'd be ready to charge the gates or go home whimpering.

There are three keys in the above passage of scripture that I want to point out.

First of all, notice that the positioning of the ark, (which represents God's presence) is central to the people. In crossing over and encountering the first obstacle in this new season, God instructed that his presence would take a central position in the battles to come. That way, his holiness would be represented in their midst. Incidentally, holiness is not something you hear a lot about today; people would rather strive for happiness!

Notice also that there is a worship culture established from the start. Many times, we are willing to worship after the victory, but a worship culture is important in the midst of the battles as well.

The second key from this story is that supernatural solutions are available as we walk into opposition. How many times do we exhaust all practical solutions before looking at the supernatural power of God in our difficulties?

> *But Joshua commanded the people, saying, "You shall not shout nor let your voice be heard nor let a word proceed out of your mouth, until the day I tell you,*

Overcoming Opposition

'Shout!' Then you shall shout!"

Joshua 6:10

Finally, an incredible key is God's instruction to not engage in dialogue with the enemy! Can you imagine walking around those walls for six days with the taunting, trash and smack talk that must have come against them? A major tactic of the enemy is to sow accusation, doubt, insecurity, and hurl the failures and regrets of our past at us without ceasing or mercy. We spend precious time engaging in battles that have no spoils to be won. It does no good to argue with the enemy, especially one who is already defeated. (He just doesn't know it yet.)

> *Then I heard a loud voice in heaven, saying, "Now the salvation, and the power, and the kingdom of our God and the authority of His Christ have come, for the accuser of our brethren has been thrown down, he who accuses them before our God day and night."*

Revelation 12:10

There is a practiced strategy that is released against believers. It is accusation. How many of us like it when that whispered voice comes against us? It's easy to hear and hard to ignore. God uses people, but so does the enemy. In fact, Peter was rebuked by Jesus at one point because he allowed the devil to use him.

> *But He turned and said to Peter, "Get behind Me, Satan! You are a stumbling block to Me; for you are not setting your mind on God's interests, but man's."*

Matthew 16:23

We cannot listen to the accusations and taunts of the enemy because that leads to doubt, fear, and the inability to overcome strongholds. We see in Joshua 6 that there are essential keys to overcoming strongholds in our lives, and the greatest breakthroughs are in front of our staunchest foes. Joshua 6 is a prophetic picture of the overcoming Christian.

Numbers are significant in the Bible. Therefore, I'm certain there is a good reason God said to march seven times, and not six or eight or forty-four. I'm not going to go into an extensive numerology study here, but let's take a quick look.

They were instructed to walk around the walls seven times, with seven priests, seven trumpets and seven blasts. Interestingly, it took seven years to subdue the land after they crossed, and there were seven nations to overcome.

Biblically we know that creation was complete on the seventh day. Thus the number seven represents completeness or perfection. The word *finished* is also connected with the number seven. The word *created* is used seven times in connection with God's work. The high priest sprinkled blood on the mercy seat seven times on the Day of Atonement, again representing completeness in the redemptive works of God. The candlestick in the holy place of the tabernacle had seven branches, and this represents the completeness in the light of God for man's soul. The blessings of the Lord are promised to his people seven times in the book of Revelation. Even medical science shows that life operates in a cycle of sevens. Every seven years, changes occur in our body, which is kind of scary! There are seven bones in our face, neck, ankle and there are seven holes in our head. (A bowling ball only has three.) In Revelation, the mystery of God is completed in the seventh vial of the seventh trumpet of the seventh seal. There are seven parables of Matthew. There are seven mysteries. There are seven

Overcoming Opposition

eternal things in Hebrews.

Do you think God likes the number seven?

All of this speaks not only to obedience but to a supernatural intersection of our lives with the Kingdom of God. In a word: Destiny! Joshua walked with real events, real people, real problems, and real victory as the people walked in obedience. There is no doubt that obedience to God in all areas of our lives is the key to overcoming obstacles and obtaining blessing. Joshua was being asked by God to be obedient to an unconventional method of warfare. And through faith and obedience those walls came down and they were able to enter into the Promise Land!

> *But in all these things we overwhelmingly conquer through Him who loved us.*
>
> Romans 8:37

Questions to Ponder

- Do I recognize the importance of obedience in obtaining victory?
- How have I dialogued with the enemy in the past?
- Is God central in my life?

Wholehearted - The Crossing

26

Testimony That Changes History

Now Joshua the son of Nun sent out two men from Acacia Grove to spy secretly, saying, "Go, view the land, especially Jericho." So they went, and came to the house of a harlot named Rahab, and lodged there.

Joshua 2:1 (NKJV)

The story of Rahab in Joshua 2 is a great example of the redemption of God. Joshua sent out two spies into a dark, wicked culture, and a great redemption came from it, displaying God's heart and willingness to use people that others would deem unfit. As such, Joshua was a foreshadowing of Jesus, exhibiting the grace that would someday cleanse all who believed.

Many of us today feel stuck in the middle of one of those dark, pagan places, perhaps a difficult job or a stressful situation where we need encouragement to hope for the restorative work of God. When we find ourselves in the midst of a Jericho, we can take heart. God has a plan!

Joshua sent two spies who ended up lodging at a brothel.

Meanwhile, the King of Jericho heard about the spies, so Rahab the prostitute hid them on her roof.

> *⁸ Now before they lay down, she came up to them on the roof, ⁹ and said to the men: "I know that the Lord has given you the land, that the terror of you has fallen on us, and that all the inhabitants of the land are fainthearted because of you. ¹⁰ For we have heard how the Lord dried up the water of the Red Sea for you when you came out of Egypt, and what you did to the two kings of the Amorites who were on the other side of the Jordan, Sihon and Og, whom you utterly destroyed. ¹¹ And as soon as we heard these things, our hearts melted; neither did there remain any more courage in anyone because of you, for the Lord your God, He is God in heaven above and on earth beneath.*
>
> Joshua 2:8-11 (NKJV)

In recounting the miraculous events preceding Israel's arrival in Jericho, Rahab saw an opportunity for salvation for her and her family. What can we learn from this? When in a strange town, find lodging in a brothel? Um…no! Seriously, when we are crossing over into something new, our testimony comes with us. Nothing speaks clearer than our reputation as people of God. We are those who believe in an almighty creator who delivers us. As Christians, we bear witness of who God is, what God stands for, how God is moving, and the amazing things God is doing. We create a sound carrying across rivers and mountains of doubt, objections, fear and skepticism, melting hard hearts to begin trusting in God. Our testimony is important to God!

Testimony That Changes History

Exodus speaks of the "ark of testimony" and the "tent of testimony," recounting the power of these places.

> *The law of the Lord is perfect, converting the soul; The testimony of the Lord is sure, making wise the simple;*
>
> Psalm 19:7 (NKJV)

> *For He established a testimony in Jacob, and appointed a law in Israel, which He commanded our fathers, that they should make them known to their children;*
>
> Psalm 78:5 (NKJV)

> *Blessed are those who keep His testimonies, who seek Him with the whole heart!*
>
> Psalm 119:2 (NKJV)

> *I have rejoiced in the way of Your testimonies, as much as in all riches.*
>
> Psalm 119:14 (NKJV)

> *Remove from me reproach and contempt, for I have kept Your testimonies.*
>
> Psalm 119:22 (NKJV)

> *Your testimonies also are my delight and my counselors.*
>
> Psalm 119:24 (NKJV)

> *I cling to Your testimonies; O Lord, do not put me to shame!*
>
> Psalm 119:31 (NKJV)

> *I will speak of Your testimonies also before kings, and will not be ashamed.*
>
> Psalm 119:46 (NKJV)

> *I have more understanding than all my teachers, for Your testimonies are my meditation.*
>
> Psalm 119:99 (NKJV)

> *And with great power the apostles gave witness to the resurrection of the Lord Jesus. And great grace was upon them all.*
>
> Acts 4:33 (NKJV)

> *Therefore do not be ashamed of the testimony of our Lord, nor of me His prisoner, but share with me in the sufferings for the gospel according to the power of God,*
>
> 2 Timothy 1:8 (NKJV)

> *And they overcame him by the blood of the Lamb and by the word of their testimony, and they did not love their lives to the death.*
>
> Revelation 12:11 (NKJV)

Obviously, testimonies are important not only as remembrances but also as tools of warfare, transformation and faith. They start as: "An oral or written declaration of what is seen," (Eaerdman's Bible Handbook). Yet they accomplish much more. Somehow, Rahab had heard the testimony of what God had been doing. She believed it and it melted her heart.

> *And as soon as we heard these things, our hearts melted; neither did there remain any more courage in*

Testimony That Changes History

> *anyone because of you, for the Lord your God, He is God in heaven above and on earth beneath.*
>
> Joshua 2:11 (NKJV)

Rahab was led in her heart by faith to receive God and obey his prompting, resulting in salvation for her and her family. She hid the spies and tied a scarlet cord in her window so her house could be saved. This was symbolic of the Passover blood applied to the doorpost during the exodus, and a harbinger of the blood of Jesus for salvation. Even though Rahab is identified as a harlot, she foreshadows the people God loves and uses in amazing ways.

Of course, Rahab didn't start out in life dreaming of working in a brothel. It's also unlikely her parents dreamed that for her. Unfortunately, she was trapped in cultural circumstances where her only hope was divine rescue from God. Consequently, when she met the spies and knew their testimony, she was ready. Hungry and desperate, she knew how to help the spies and so responded in faith to the opportunity before her to obey God.

Faith and obedience to God will change our destiny, overcome our history, leave a legacy, and preserve the future of our family. Rahab knew that Jericho was about to undergo the judgment of God, and she realized the hopeless future for her city. Something changed, however, when she believed the testimony of our amazing God and gave her life to him. Consequently, she is honored in the books of Matthew, Hebrews and James. The book of Matthew lists her in the genealogy of Jesus, as she was the wife of Salmon who was the son of Boaz that married Ruth and thus the grandfather of David.

> *5 Salmon begot Boaz by Rahab, Boaz begot Obed by Ruth, Obed begot Jesse, 6 and Jesse begot David the*

> *king. David the king begot Solomon by her who had been the wife of Uriah.*
>
> Matthew 1:5-6 (NKJV)

She is included in the "hall of faith" in Hebrews.

> *By faith the harlot Rahab did not perish with those who did not believe, when she had received the spies with peace.*
>
> Hebrews 11:31 (NKJV)

Similarly, she is honored in James.

> *[23] And the Scripture was fulfilled which says, "Abraham believed God, and it was accounted to him for righteousness." And he was called the friend of God. [24] You see then that a man is justified by works, and not by faith only. [25] Likewise, was not Rahab the harlot also justified by works when she received the messengers and sent them out another way?*
>
> James 2:23-25 (NKJV)

Amazingly, and to the credit of God's love, she is listed right after Abraham! This story illustrates powerfully that God is still looking for the Rahab's of our world! God sent Joshua into Jericho to overcome and possess the city, but God's heart was also looking for Rahab and those like her!

There are people like Rahab all around us. They are captured, enslaved, and in need of rescue. They need your testimony of how God has saved you, redeemed you, and changed your destiny. The faith you live by is the sound that will melt hard hearts, allowing hope and faith to rise within them.

> *[1] Oh, give thanks to the Lord, for He is good! For His*

Testimony That Changes History

> *mercy endures forever. ² Let the redeemed of the Lord say so, whom He has redeemed from the hand of the enemy,*
>
> Psalm 107:1-2 (NKJV)

Just as there are people like Rahab, so there is some of her in all of us. When presented with the opportunity to respond with faith and obedience to Christ, it changes our destiny for our lives and those we love.

Questions to Ponder:

- How is my testimony preceding me?
- Do I recognize that God is always looking for the Rahabs of the world?
- How great of a factor is faith and obedience in my life?

Wholehearted - The Crossing

27

The Achan In All Of Us

¹⁵ Then on the seventh day they rose early at the dawning of the day and marched around the city in the same manner seven times; only on that day they marched around the city seven times. ¹⁶ At the seventh time, when the priests blew the trumpets, Joshua said to the people, "Shout! For the Lord has given you the city.

Joshua 6:15-16

Most men I know typically don't like authority. Charles Finney spoke of obedience and sacrifice, saying: *"Revival is nothing more or less than a new obedience to God!"*

Joshua 6 speaks of obedience, its success and failure. To be candid, we have to admit that disobedience comes naturally to us; it's in our old nature and saturates the fallen world. There is something alluring about being disobedient—rebels with or without a cause. We all have some rebel in us. We thrill at the sound of the rebel yell, cheer sports teams named The Rebels, and absorbing stories of iconoclasts and insurgents thwarting the course of evil empires—rebels of a nobler sort. From the sandbox declaration of "You're not the boss of me" to questioning the State Trooper as to why in the world some *idiot* set the speed limit at 55 instead of 90 on this long, lonely stretch of highway. (Well, maybe not so lonely.)

Which is why Israel's God-given victory over Jericho was so difficult. This was not a typical military campaign! These were fighting men, men of war, battle hardened and wilderness strong. Some had even read my book! They were ready to take the city by force, but a march and a trumpet serenade? *We sharpened our swords for this?*

It is always a test of trust and obedience when God's ways are unusual.

> *³ For though we walk in the flesh, we do not war according to the flesh. ⁴ For the weapons of our warfare are not carnal but mighty in God for pulling down strongholds, ⁵ casting down arguments and every high thing that exalts itself against the knowledge of God, bringing every thought into captivity to the obedience of Christ, ⁶ and being ready to punish all disobedience when your obedience is fulfilled.*
>
> 2 Corinthians 10:3-6 (NKJV)

It reminds me of Peter in the garden. You have to love him. Carrying a sword to defend the King of Kings. Problem was, he missed the mark and hit the ear. (I think he was swinging for the guy's head). Jesus had put the poor guy's ear back on! Well, at least Peter was swinging at something!

Peter would have done well to study the overcoming of Jericho. It is a lesson in the blessing of faith in God—not just in the assault of the city, but in the aftermath as well. See Joshua's specific

The Achan In All Of Us

instructions for the after-victory party.

> *"But all the silver and gold and articles of bronze and iron are holy to the Lord; they shall go into the treasury of the Lord."*
>
> Joshua 6:19

Prior to the assault on Jericho, God was very specific about the blessings of obedience. This is the famous passage from the teachings of Moses in which he lays out perfectly for the people of Israel the blessings of obeying God.

> [1] *"Now it shall come to pass, if you diligently obey the voice of the Lord your God, to observe carefully all His commandments which I command you today, that the Lord your God will set you high above all nations of the earth.* [2] *And all these blessings shall come upon you and overtake you, because you obey the voice of the Lord your God:* [3] *Blessed shall you be in the city, and blessed shall you be in the country.* [4] *Blessed shall be the fruit of your body, the produce of your ground and the increase of your herds, the increase of your cattle and the offspring of your flocks.* [5] *Blessed shall be your basket and your kneading bowl.* [6] *Blessed shall you be when you come in, and blessed shall you be when you go out.* [7] *The Lord will cause your enemies who rise against you to be defeated before your face; they shall come out against you one way and flee before you seven ways.* [8] *The Lord will command the blessing on you in your storehouses and in all to which you set your hand, and He will bless you in the land which the Lord your*

God is giving you. ⁹ "The Lord will establish you as a holy people to Himself, just as He has sworn to you, if you keep the commandments of the Lord your God and walk in His ways. ¹⁰ Then all peoples of the earth shall see that you are called by the name of the Lord, and they shall be afraid of you. ¹¹ And the Lord will grant you plenty of goods, in the fruit of your body, in the increase of your livestock, and in the produce of your ground, in the land of which the Lord swore to your fathers to give you. ¹² The Lord will open to you His good treasure, the heavens, to give the rain to your land in its season, and to bless all the work of your hand. You shall lend to many nations, but you shall not borrow. ¹³ And the Lord will make you the head and not the tail; you shall be above only, and not be beneath, if you heed the commandments of the Lord your God, which I command you today, and are careful to observe them. ¹⁴ So you shall not turn aside from any of the words which I command you this day, to the right or the left, to go after other gods to serve them."

Deuteronomy 28:1-14 (NKJV)

Of course, the Lord knows what people are like, so he went on in Deuteronomy 28:15-68 to describe the consequences if the men were disobedient. Hopefully the point is clear: Obedience is a HUGE deal in being a Christian. Jesus put it succinctly: *"If you love me, you will obey my commandments"* (John 14: 15).

Obedience couldn't have been more critical as Joshua moved his people into the Promised Land full of milk and honey. Just as

The Achan In All Of Us

today, the greatest opposition stands before the greatest blessing. Earlier, we saw two ways that God called Israel to be obedient in the conquest of Jericho. It was in how they walked and in how they talked. We see further in Joshua 6-7 instruction on obedience in stewardship and separation.

> *[18] And you, by all means abstain from the accursed things, lest you become accursed when you take of the accursed things, and make the camp of Israel a curse, and trouble it. [19] But all the silver and gold, and vessels of bronze and iron, are consecrated to the Lord; they shall come into the treasury of the Lord."*
>
> Joshua 6:18-19 (NKJV)

Now here is the separation of action and obedience, and the consequences for Israel.

> *But the children of Israel committed a trespass regarding the accursed things, for Achan the son of Carmi, the son of Zabdi, the son of Zerah, of the tribe of Judah, took of the accursed things; so the anger of the Lord burned against the children of Israel.*
>
> Joshua 7:1 (NKJV)

> *[19] Now Joshua said to Achan, "My son, I beg you, give glory to the Lord God of Israel, and make confession to Him, and tell me now what you have done; do not hide it from me." [20] And Achan answered Joshua and said, "Indeed I have sinned against the Lord God of Israel, and this is what I have done: [21] When I saw among the spoils a beautiful Babylonian garment, two hundred shekels of silver, and a wedge of gold weighing fifty shekels, I coveted them and took them.*

> *And there they are, hidden in the earth in the midst of my tent, with the silver under it."*
>
> Joshua 7:19-21 (NKJV)

Now if you follow the story, Israel gained a great victory against Jericho, but problems arose when they went to subdue Ai, a much smaller and weaker city. It should not have been a problem, except disobedience reared its ugly head! A man named Achan disobeyed the instructions given and hoarded some of the loot.

Jericho was the first of seven cities and seven nations that Israel would go into to subdue, and it is the only one that God said to bring all the finances into the treasure of the Lord. I believe (along with many scholars) that this was a type of tithe. God has always reserved a certain portion for himself, to be dedicated to the things of God. When Israel conquered Ai and the cities after Jericho, they were allowed to keep all the spoils of battle, but Achan ignored the message. The result was a resounding defeat in the battle at Ai and the death of several dozen warriors, none of whom had sinned individually. But because of Achan, Israel was accursed.

ACCURSED: Translation of Hebrew *cherem*, a technical term in warfare for items captured from the enemy and devoted to God.

In Malachi, God confronted his people, saying they had robbed him of tithes and offerings. Jesus spoke of the tithe and it was recorded both in the gospel of Matthew and Luke.

> *"Woe to you, scribes and Pharisees, hypocrites! For you pay tithe of mint and anise and cummin, and have neglected the weightier matters of the law: justice and mercy and faith. These you ought to have done, without leaving the others undone."*

The Achan In All Of Us

Matthew 23:23 (NKJV)

"But woe to you Pharisees! For you tithe mint and rue and all manner of herbs, and pass by justice and the love of God. These you ought to have done, without leaving the others undone."

Luke 11:42 (NKJV)

Honor the Lord with your possessions, And with the firstfruits of all your increase;

Proverbs 3:9 (NKJV)

It's also important to note that Jesus never lowered the bar; instead, he always upped it! For example, look at the Old Covenant vs. New Covenant when it comes to marriage issues.

> [27] *"You have heard that it was said to those of old, 'You shall not commit adultery.'* [28] *But I say to you that whoever looks at a woman to lust for her has already committed adultery with her in his heart."*

Matthew 5:27-28 (NKJV)

So in the taking of new territory, Achan had violated the principle of stewarding the money as God had instructed. (*Always follow the money.*)

The other thing Achan did wrong was to take a Babylonian garment—a beautiful dress. The problem is that it represented the very thing God did not want Israel to be. If God had wanted his people to resemble Babylonians, he would have left Abraham there. If God wanted his people to resemble Egypt, he would have left his people in Egypt. Instead, God called his people out, sanctifying them and marking them, calling them his own, and thus pronouncing them Holy. Achan's sin was not only touching the portion of money that God called his own, but also in bringing the very thing that God was trying to deliver them from back into his home, his family and his culture.

In truth, the Achan in all of us is tempted to do that very thing. Aside from stewardship, we know we should love, forgive, and repent of sins that destroy not only the fabric of relationship, but are opposite of the core values of the Kingdom of God. We also are tempted to harbor things in our lives that God has delivered us from! While the particular sins are unique to our personalities—don't ask me how I feel when I hear Eric Clapton playing guitar—the results are universal. It's impossible to bring in a little sin and not have it permeate through everything we touch.

Of course, on the other side of the obedience issue, there is legalism. I've been in situations where the "clothesline" has been preached and enforced: what clothes to wear, what haircuts to get, how much jewelry, makeup and perfume to wear. Really? Lacking proficiency with the inner workings of the heart, we easily resort to an external form of godliness. Such thinking also spills over to our theology with arguments on whether Gentiles should still obey the laws of Moses, or whether the moral part of the mosaic covenant is the only thing that should be upheld. Legalism leaves many wounded and abused, especially those honestly trying to obey it as a pure endeavor to follow God. In the end, legalism only diminishes the blessing and call of obedience as a follower of Jesus. Again, Jesus said that if we love him, we will obey his commands. That obedience draws us into a deep place of blessing from God. And I think we can figure out how long our hair should be.

Despite Achan's sin, God had some amazing promises ahead for Joshua and the people, things that were already accomplished in

The Achan In All Of Us

God's mind, waiting to be materialized as the bridges of obedience were built and faithfully crossed. In truth, God has great things for all of us.

> "For I know the plans that I have for you," declares the Lord, "plans for welfare and not for calamity to give you a future and a hope.
>
> Jeremiah 29:11

God yearns to bless us as we learn to overcome, obey and walk in faith. The fact of the matter is, however, that he must first qualify us before he can bless us. To do otherwise would destroy us. Thus, we are to strive for obedience:

- obedience in how we walk
- obedience in how we talk
- obedience in how we steward the God-given resources of time, treasure and talent.

Questions to Ponder:

- In what areas of my life is God is calling me to obey him?
- Where have I been blessed by obedience?
- What areas of my life are the toughest for me to walk in faith?

Wholehearted - The Crossing

28

Back to the Tent!

² Now Joshua sent men from Jericho to Ai, which is near Bethaven, east of Bethel, and said to them, "Go up and spy out the land." So the men went up and spied out Ai. ³ They returned to Joshua and said to him, "Do not let all the people go up; only about two or three thousand men need go up to Ai; do not make all the people toil up there, for they are few." ⁴ So about three thousand men from the people went up there, but they fled from the men of Ai. ⁵ The men of Ai struck down about thirty-six of their men, and pursued them from the gate as far as Shebarim and struck them down on the descent, so the hearts of the people melted and became as water.

Joshua 7:2-5

With the battle of Ai, Joshua entered a new season, one of dealing with the difficulty of defeat. Even as Joshua and Israel moved into the new season of realized promises, they had a lot to learn, much like us!

Where do you go in defeat? What is your reaction to loss. How do you deal with the sting of condemnation and the conviction that you missed the mark? We are not created for defeat, but to be *"more than conquerors through Christ"* (Romans 8:37). Yet the reality of life means there are times when we misstep, make mistakes and sin. Certainly there is a sting of shame and condemnation, and often consequences, but we must get beyond it.

Who enjoys defeat? Who likes to lose? Whether it's a card game, a race, a rock-skipping contest, the normal desire is to come out first. In my athletic days, I got to coach basketball for a few years. That's when I learned that the thrill of victory was closely accompanied by the agony of defeat. We tend to measure our life by successes, hoping that in the end, the ledger will list more victories than failures. And when we think about it, who remembers the loser of the championship fight, or the team that *nearly* won the Super Bowl *four times in a row*. (Sorry Buffalo fans.) Although I've learned a lot through my success, I've learned far more through my failures.

We are created to win—I believe that with all my heart. What healthy father desires his son to just get by in life? Yet defeats are part of life, and in these verses above, Joshua and the people are feeling the consequences of losing. This was their first defeat since entering into the Promised Land. They had lost 36 men in a fight that should have been easy. What's worse, however, was that they had lost confidence in themselves and God, fearing that word would eventually reach their enemies and embolden them to attack.

The interaction between God and Joshua, and subsequently the response of Joshua, can teach us some critical things about our responses to failure.

Back to the Tent!

> *Now the Lord said to Joshua, "Do not fear or be dismayed. Take all the people of war with you and arise, go up to Ai; see, I have given into your hand the king of Ai, his people, his city, and his land.*
>
> Joshua 8:1

This passage gives us an important key. *"Now the Lord said to Joshua."* In looking back in scripture, it is interesting to note that nowhere in the initial conquest of Ai had Joshua or the leaders inquired of God! Because they had overcome Jericho, a much more formidable opponent, they basically said, *"We got this."* (I personally don't think this defeat was all Achan's fault!)

In the aftermath of Achan's sin, the dialogue between Joshua and God speaks to the need to get back to the tent, the place where Joshua met with God and God met with Joshua! Joshua's first step in recovering from defeat was reconnecting with God at the tent of meeting.

> *Thus the Lord used to speak to Moses face to face, just as a man speaks to his friend. When Moses returned to the camp, his servant Joshua, the son of Nun, a young man, would not depart from the tent.*
>
> Exodus 33:11

Communion with God is what made Joshua different. It is what made Joshua see with faith. It is what qualified Joshua! And it is what restored Joshua. The tent of meeting symbolized God's presence; it was there that Joshua was forged, changed, impacted and empowered.

Consider a tent. It is comprised of five things.

- Roof—speaks of government

- Sides—speaks of structure, boundaries
- Floor—speaks of building your house on the rock
- Supports—speaks of community, fellowship, the church
- Door—speaks of entry, of decisions

Many times after defeat, we hide in shame from the very things that can help us recover: the atmosphere of worship, the fellowship of other Christians, and the governance of the Holy Spirit and the Word. Adam sinned, suffered defeat, and the first action he took was to hide from God!

We have to get beyond the patterns endemic to our carnal nature.

- When you suffer defeat, get back to the tent.
- When you want to be an overcomer, get back to the tent.
- To get back on track, get back to the tent.

Essentially…GET BACK TO THE TENT!

Another lesson Joshua learned in moving forward from Ai was to take counsel from the right people.

> *²Now Joshua sent men from Jericho to Ai, which is near Beth-aven, east of Bethel, and said to them, "Go up and spy out the land." So the men went up and spied out Ai. ³They returned to Joshua and said to him, "Do not let all the people go up; only about two or three thousand men need go up to Ai; do not make all the people toil up there, for they are few."*
>
> Joshua 7:2-3

Back to the Tent!

Just as he had seen Moses do, Joshua sent in spies, but they needed to be the right spies who would offer the right advice. In this case, their over-confident advice couldn't have been more wrong. *"We got this,"* quickly devolved into *"They got us."*

In my earlier testimony on my upbringing, I wrote that my mom had a love for God coupled with a horrible track record with marriage. I love her. She was wise in many areas, but in the area of marriage, I would not seek her counsel!

In regards to Joshua and the counsel he sought, these were not "tent of the meeting" guys. Solomon writes: *"There is wisdom in a multitude of counsel"* (Proverbs 15:22). But we had better judge the sources of that advice. I want to take counsel from people who have that "tent of meeting" spirit to them! Soaking in the presence of God adds wholeness that conveys spiritual wisdom and power.

For example, a young preacher once delivered an incredibly inspirational message. Two elderly ladies in the congregation conferred afterward. "What did you think about that young preacher's sermon?" one of the ladies asked the other. "He will be a lot better after he has suffered for a while," the other replied. I would not encourage that preacher to take those ladies' advice.

There is a need for wise counsel—the demarcation between failure and success.

> *15 This wisdom is not that which comes down from above, but is earthly, natural, demonic. 16 For where jealousy and selfish ambition exist, there is disorder and every evil thing. 17 But the wisdom from above is first pure, then peaceable, gentle, reasonable, full of mercy and good fruits, unwavering, without hypocrisy.*
>
> James 3:15-17

Finally, the story of Ai also highlights a mistake that we all make time and time again, that of underestimating the enemy. Certainly we don't *overestimate* him either, but too many people forget the whole armor of God.

> *Be of sober spirit, be on the alert. Your adversary, the devil, prowls around like a roaring lion, seeking someone to devour.*
>
> 1 Peter 5:8

> *… and they may come to their senses and escape from the snare of the devil, having been held captive by him to do his will.*
>
> 2 Timothy 2:26

Ever see a cat hunt? Kind of chilling as they lurk patiently. The only sign of life from their frozen form is the small twitch of tail as they wait for their prey to make a fatal mistake. Snares work the same way. Snares of addiction, bitterness, unforgiveness, complaint, lust, stupidity, pride, arrogance, isolation…so many. Without wise counsel, we are the next mouse between the cat's claws.

Joshua finally reconnected with the Lord, and God gave him counsel saying, *"Do not fear or be dismayed. Take all the people of war with you and arise, go up to Ai"* (Joshua 8:1). Time to make a statement; time to not underestimate the foe; time to win in spades.

Winston Churchill had this advice for West Point graduates: *Never give up.* God spoke to Joshua and said, *"See, I have given into your hand the king of Ai, his people, his city, and his land"* (Joshua 8:1).

You may feel as though you have failed, maybe even been

Back to the Tent!

defeated too many times. So what? Never give up. In the mind of God it is not over!

As people of God, we are not guaranteed freedom from setbacks. In fact, we can expect some defeats. But the Bible says, *"We are more than conquerors in Christ Jesus"* (Romans 8:37). God gives us instruction, armor, strategies, and wise counsel, all in the tent of meeting.

Get back to the tent. Take counsel from the right people. Don't underestimate the enemy.

NEVER GIVE UP!

Questions to Ponder

- What is my reaction to defeat?
- What is my criteria for seeking out counsel?
- What does it mean to be alert for the enemy?

Wholehearted - The Crossing

29

Facing Your Failure

3 When the inhabitants of Gibeon heard what Joshua had done to Jericho and to Ai, 4 they also acted craftily and set out as envoys, and took worn-out sacks on their donkeys, and wineskins worn-out and torn and mended, 5 and worn-out and patched sandals on their feet, and worn-out clothes on themselves; and all the bread of their provision was dry and had become crumbled. 6 They went to Joshua to the camp at Gilgal and said to him and to the men of Israel, "We have come from a far country; now therefore, make a covenant with us."

Joshua 9:3-6

In order to recover from defeat, we first have to acknowledge it. Like Joshua, we have to face being overconfident, getting the wrong type of counsel, and the consequences of sin on the entire group. (See previous chapter.)

Everyone makes mistakes; that's a given. It's our commitment to move forward out of failure that is the launching pad for God to move us forward into something new and fresh! Too easy to dwell on past defeats. Our steps forward are a powerful measure of recovery. In the passage above, we find that once again, the enemy was cunning and Joshua was deceived. You will note, however, that he must have learned something, for his recovery was stunning.

The issue centered around God directing Israel not to sign any treaties with the nations they were invading, because God knew these nations were opposed to him. Ultimately, through the bond they forged, they would lead Israel away from God and into idolatry.

When we make that covenant relationship with God, we cross over into the new season. There will be the temptation to fall back into old stuff, old alliances, unequally yoked relationships. And Joshua FAILED! AGAIN! He fell into sin...again!

Strange as this may sound, this story is encouraging to me because it is about real people that God loves and uses, and yet they mess up all the time much as you and I do! We are good at creating messes. We all know our children are better at tearing things up than putting them back together. When we occasionally see one of them picking things up and organizing, we want celebrate! And when our teenagers do it, we immediately become suspicious! What do they want?!

The Bible is full of men and women who were favored by God; their only qualification *seems* to be that they were flawed and failed a lot! Ah, the mercy, grace and redemptive nature of our God! Some of the biggest failures come after the greatest victories, and the greatest victories come after the biggest failures...if we respond well.

> *6They went to Joshua to the camp at Gilgal and said to him and to the men of Israel, "We have come from*

Facing Your Failure

a far country; now therefore, make a covenant with us." ⁷The men of Israel said to the Hivites, "Perhaps you are living within our land; how then shall we make a covenant with you?" ⁸But they said to Joshua, "We are your servants." Then Joshua said to them, "Who are you and where do you come from?" ⁹They said to him, "Your servants have come from a very far country because of the fame of the Lord your God; for we have heard the report of Him and all that He did in Egypt, ¹⁰and all that He did to the two kings of the Amorites who were beyond the Jordan, to Sihon king of Heshbon and to Og king of Bashan who was at Ashtaroth. ¹¹"So our elders and all the inhabitants of our country spoke to us, saying, 'Take provisions in your hand for the journey, and go to meet them and say to them, "We are your servants; now then, make a covenant with us."' ¹²"This our bread was warm when we took it for our provisions out of our houses on the day that we left to come to you; but now behold, it is dry and has become crumbled. ¹³"These wineskins which we filled were new, and behold, they are torn; and these our clothes and our sandals are worn out because of the very long journey." ¹⁴So the men of Israel took some of their provisions, and did not ask for the counsel of the Lord. ¹⁵Joshua made peace with them and made a covenant with them, to let them live; and the leaders of the congregation swore an oath to them. ¹⁶It came about at the end of three days after they had made a covenant with them, that they heard that they were neighbors and that they were living within their land.

Joshua 9:6-16

So Joshua had been tricked into forming an alliance that God specifically instructed him to avoid. I think there may have been a couple reasons for Joshua's mistake.

> *Now it came about when all the kings who were beyond the Jordan, in the hill country and in the lowland and on all the coast of the Great Sea toward Lebanon, the Hittite and the Amorite, the Canaanite, the Perizzite, the Hivite and the Jebusite, heard of it,*
>
> Joshua 9:1

It started when all the other kings *"heard about"* Israel's fighting prowess. Unfortunately, Joshua was vulnerable; he forgot the old maxim (well, it wasn't so old back then; probably not even invented yet): "Never read your own press." Certainly, it would not be the first time that men were overconfident, self-reliant, cocky and a little foolish. This is the same group who underestimated Ai, after all.

The problem with successes is that it can go to our heads, trip us up and become a downfall. We forget that *"God opposes the proud but gives grace to the humble"* (James 4:6), and so we let down our guard. We forget as well the ability of the devil to deceive.

> *"You are of your father the devil, and you want to do the desires of your father. He was a murderer from the beginning, and does not stand in the truth because there is no truth in him. Whenever he speaks a lie, he speaks from his own nature, for he is a liar and the father of lies.*
>
> John 8:44

Facing Your Failure

And the devil who deceived them was thrown into the lake of fire and brimstone, where the beast and the false prophet are also; and they will be tormented day and night forever and ever.

Revelation 20:10

So that no advantage would be taken of us by Satan, for we are not ignorant of his schemes.

2 Corinthians 2:11

But the Spirit explicitly says that in later times some will fall away from the faith, paying attention to deceitful spirits and doctrines of demons,

1 Timothy 4:1

We live in a culture where spirits of deception and doctrines of demons are a reality—a season where the discernment of the Holy Spirit in the life of a believer has never been more important! Joshua was vulnerable to deception after victories over Jericho and Ai. He was primed for failure by his success. Notice the sense of self-sufficiency among the warriors.

So the men of Israel took some of their provisions, and did not ask for the counsel of the Lord.

Joshua 9:14

Once again, we see that they failed to consider God's counsel in the matter. If they had asked, God would have revealed the deception.

Why don't we ask for God's counsel? Do we sense that what we want is not what God wants? Is it easier to ask forgiveness than permission? Probably all of that and more. Paul writes, *"pray without ceasing"* (I Thessalonians 5:17). We need the counsel of

God to walk in a wholesome and healthy way.

This was how Joshua failed. But here's how he recovered by confronting the enemy.

> *Then Joshua called for them and spoke to them, saying, "Why have you deceived us, saying, 'We are very far from you,' when you are living within our land?*
>
> Joshua 9:22

The first key to allowing God to redeem our failure is to confront it. We need to admit it and repent of it. Sometimes we don't confront the reason why we failed for fear that God won't like us anymore. The truth is that God is faithful; he can take our messes, our failures, and if we submit to him, he will make something redemptive out of them!

The second key is to take ownership and continue to walk in integrity. Two wrongs don't make a right. We can't resort to flesh to get us out of a situation that flesh got us into. In our story, although Israel had been deceived, they kept their word to Gibeon and submitted to the Lord. It would have been far easier in the short term to just destroy the Gibeonites and have it done with, but Israel did not compound their failure by adding another to it! God rewards integrity. We find that later the Gibeonites, under Ezra and Nehemiah, were given the title *"Nethinim"* which means "the given ones." They were given to the priests for service at the temple and gradually accepted God themselves. Further, one of David's mighty men was a Gibeonite, and Nehemiah records that there were Gibeonites who helped rebuild the walls of Jerusalem. Although the Gibeonites deceived Joshua, turning the whole thing over to God ultimately resulted in the redemption of the deceivers!

Facing Your Failure

Men and women of favor in the Bible were not perfect, but the measure of their lives was in their correct responses to failure.

What is your mess? Your failure, misstep or sin? If you can confront it, repent of it, and walk with integrity through it, you can also see the redemptive grace of God unfold no matter what the situation.

Questions to Ponder

- Have I turned my failures over to God?
- Have I walked with integrity through them?
- What are some victories I have realized from facing my mistakes squarely?

Wholehearted - The Crossing

30

Kings of Opposition

> *1Now it came about when Adonizedek king of Jerusalem heard that Joshua had captured Ai, and had utterly destroyed it (just as he had done to Jericho and its king, so he had done to Ai and its king), and that the inhabitants of Gibeon had made peace with Israel and were within their land, 2 that he feared greatly, because Gibeon was a great city, like one of the royal cities, and because it was greater than Ai, and all its men were mighty.*
>
> Joshua 10:1-2

As a child, no one taught me about the reality of opposition. Resistance is not one of those things parents typically teach as a core value. Instead, we learn it from life itself, beginning somewhere between the sandbox and adulthood. Opposition and resistance are inevitable, and our response each time it confronts us prepares us for the next level and the next lesson.

Resistance can be an incredibly healthy experience. Take lifting weights as an example. Without resistance there is no strength gained. This is why the lack of gravity to an astronaut does funky things physically that must be overcome.

The determining factor for benefitting from opposition is in how we face it and walk through it. It can destroy us or strengthen us; either way, it will define us. Character is challenged in our response to opposition, be it in spiritual realms, family relationships, or physical challenges.

In the passage above, Israel is now facing its greatest opposition. Jericho and Ai were lessons but nothing compared to what faced them now. There were now five kings and five armies, and even though Israel ultimately defeated Ai, the fact that it took two tries had given their enemies hope.

> *3 Therefore Adoni-zedek king of Jerusalem sent word to Hoham king of Hebron and to Piram king of Jarmuth and to Japhia king of Lachish and to Debir king of Eglon, saying, 4 "Come up to me and help me, and let us attack Gibeon, for it has made peace with Joshua and with the sons of Israel." 5 So the five kings of the Amorites, the king of Jerusalem, the king of Hebron, the king of Jarmuth, the king of Lachish, and the king of Eglon, gathered together and went up, they with all their armies, and camped by Gibeon and fought against it.*
>
> Joshua 10:3-5

We all face a normal level of daily opposition. However, there are also "kings of opposition." Higher levels; higher devils. We would be blown away if we could see the enemy's web of warfare assigned to shoot fiery darts against us. The Bible says that we have an enemy that comes to *"kill, steal and destroy"* (John 10:10). The devil has been practicing that strategy for a long time!

Kings of Opposition

Joshua 10 recounts one of the most incredible miracles ever recorded. Sure, the Bible has miracles of dead people raised, lame walking and blind seeing, but never has there been a miracle as we see in Joshua 10. But first, the setup.

> *⁶ Then the men of Gibeon sent word to Joshua to the camp at Gilgal, saying, "Do not abandon your servants; come up to us quickly and save us and help us, for all the kings of the Amorites that live in the hill country have assembled against us." ⁷ So Joshua went up from Gilgal, he and all the people of war with him and all the valiant warriors.*
>
> Joshua 10:6-7

The first key we see here has to do with response to this new and bigger challenge.

How we carry ourselves after we have failed has everything to do with how we recover. Remember: we are all failed, flawed success stories in God!

When facing opposition, we must maintain our integrity. We saw in the last chapter that Joshua messed up but walked through it with integrity, and here he is again, correcting his actions by honoring his word to the Gibeonites. Israel's mistake was in not consulting with God before making a treaty with the Gibeonites. However, now that they had done so, they were bound by it, even though the people under their leadership were grumbling about the treaty. It would have been the perfect opportunity to abandon Gibeon.

What commitments should you honor? Maybe you should honor that debt you owe; repay that commitment you made; address that issue you have been avoiding with a brother or sister.

Integrity as a believer speaks of being consistent in character, especially in conflict. Are you the same inside the church as you are in the world? On the job? In the home? A lack of integrity erodes relationship. It is the opposite of the character God wants to forge in us. Joshua faced this new challenge—this time a challenge to his word—and he maintained his integrity.

The second key idea is that challenges always seem to come in multiples.

We fight on several fronts. It's the nature of war. We deal with the spirit of the world, the weakness of our flesh, and own desires. Oh yeah, and the devil and his angels.

Israel was no different. At first they faced Jericho, then Ai, and now they were facing five kings with five armies defending five cities with resources behind them! Jericho and Ai were nothing compared this! Conflict on multiple fronts requires a greater grace and faith; the size of the challenge determines the size of the response. In the passage below, we see in the interaction between God and Joshua a greater provision than Joshua thought possible.

> [8] *The Lord said to Joshua, "Do not fear them, for I have given them into your hands; not one of them shall stand before you."* [9] *So Joshua came upon them suddenly by marching all night from Gilgal.* [10] *And the Lord confounded them before Israel, and He slew them with a great slaughter at Gibeon, and pursued them by the way of the ascent of Beth-horon and struck them as far as Azekah and Makkedah.* [11] *As they fled from before Israel, while they were at the descent of Beth-horon, the Lord threw large stones from heaven on them as far as Azekah, and they*

Kings of Opposition

> *died; there were more who died from the hailstones than those whom the sons of Israel killed with the sword.* ¹² *Then Joshua spoke to the Lord in the day when the Lord delivered up the Amorites before the sons of Israel, and he said in the sight of Israel, "O sun, stand still at Gibeon, And O moon in the valley of Aijalon."* ¹³ *So the sun stood still, and the moon stopped, until the nation avenged themselves of their enemies. Is it not written in the book of Jashar? And the sun stopped in the middle of the sky and did not hasten to go down for about a whole day.* ¹⁴ *There was no day like that before it or after it, when the Lord listened to the voice of a man; for the Lord fought for Israel.*
>
> Joshua 10:8-14

Notice that this time, God spoke to Joshua *before* the conflict began. Joshua, to his credit, saw the enormity of the challenge and sought God. In turn, the Lord responded with, *"I've got this,"* and the hail stones fell. It seems that Joshua learned his lesson and stayed in relationship with God. Further, notice that Joshua's failures were over relatively trivial issues compared to the overwhelming challenge he could not have foreseen. Even though his mistakes at Jericho and Ai were costly, they were mere stepping stones on the way to Israel's greatest challenge to date. He lost 36 men at Ai because he failed to consult God, but could have lost his entire army against the five kings.

We must learn to position ourselves in a way for God to speak to us, instruct and encourage us. The challenges in life get a lot easier when we know God's heart toward us.

The third key idea when facing opposition is to remember that God is for us!

> *What then shall we say to these things? If God is for us, who is against us?*
>
> Romans 8:31

> *As they fled from before Israel, while they were at the descent of Beth-horon, the Lord threw large stones from heaven on them as far as Azekah, and they died; there were more who died from the hailstones than those whom the sons of Israel killed with the sword.*
>
> Joshua 10:11

God threw large stones from heaven? What was that about? During the greatest conflict facing the fledgling nation, the Lord fought vehemently on their behalf. Let this be something we never forget. In Israel's deliverance from the captivity of Egypt, it was not Moses' prowess as a general that prevailed, but the signs, miracles and wonders of God. All Moses had to do was throw down a stick; God turned it into a snake. All Moses had to do was put his hand inside his robe; God changed the form of his flesh. All Moses had to do was speak what God told him to; God backed up the words with actions.

When did we stop believing in miracles, signs and wonders? Who says they are no longer necessary? Have we reached a point where we don't need them? In our families, in our communities, in our nation? We need them. We are living miracles, vessels inhabited by the living God. Everything flows from there.

The fourth key when facing opposition is to pray into what seems impossible.

Kings of Opposition

As Israel faced five kings and five armies, and God did battle on behalf of His people, something even more incredible happened. In the midst of this great deliverance, Joshua prayed the impossible, and God suspended the laws of nature, making the sun stand still in the sky. (He is the one who made the laws; he has the right to suspend them, don't you think?)

So was this miracle a trick of perception? Did God really lengthen the day so Israel could wreak havoc in its enemies? It is interesting to note that early Chinese history, Incan history, Egyptian and Babylonian history all record an unusually long day.

Apparently, the size of the challenge determines the size of the response! Joshua was encouraged by the Word of the Lord and his response was to pray for the impossible. Pray big or go home! The greater the challenge, the greater the prayer!

God is interested in engaging with his people. Part of that interaction is defending them. We do well to remember this when faced with impossible odds, staggering loss, or insurmountable challenges. Let these lessons engender in you the temerity to pray impossible prayers to a God for whom *"all things are possible."*

> *And looking at them Jesus said to them, "With people this is impossible, but with God all things are possible."*
>
> (Matthew 19:26)

God wants you to know he is with you. But it is necessary to position yourself to hear him as he encourages and strengthens you. It's time to pray like you've never prayed before—big prayers, impossible prayers, prayers that stretch your imagination. Opposition and resistance are realities of life, but there is only one way to walk in victory. We face challenges with divine resources at the ready.

Wholehearted - The Crossing

Questions to Ponder

- What are the main oppositions I have faced?
- How have they defined me?
- Can I pray the impossible today?

31

A Longing Fulfilled

¹³So Joshua blessed Caleb son of Jephunneh and gave Hebron to him as his portion of land.

Joshua 14:13 (NLT)

Caleb was weary. The old man ached from countless wars and encounters. His tunic and belt were stained with blood, his clothing was worn from the hardship of battle with kings and soldiers. Scars from wounds had healed, yet some remained tender, speaking to him as reminders. How many battles? How many kings? It was a blur to him as he gazed within his tent at the spoils of those fights. A collection of swords and knives, spears and slings, arrows and such. Reminders but not rewards. Not the reward that he was promised or wanted. There was a stirring outside of the tents as the men gathered around Joshua. As he joined them, Caleb's memories flooded his mind and heart. Looking upon Joshua's face, he remembered the years of wandering, the adventure of pursuing, and the regrets of delay. He saw in Joshua the same resolution that was in his heart the day they returned from spying out this new land of promise. Life was good. God was good. Enemies could be overcome. It was a wholehearted report, full of faith and expectancy. And yet the hope of it was deferred.

Until now.

It was the day of inheritance, one of reckoning and memory of words spoken. The response of his heart was suddenly at the forefront of his mind. The weariness that his body carried could not extinguish the steady burning commitment that flowed from his spirit. Caleb's eyes brightened as he caught Joshua's attention At last, Caleb began to speak.

> *9So that day Moses solemnly promised me, 'The land of Canaan on which you were just walking will be your grant of land and that of your descendants forever, because you wholeheartedly followed the Lord my God.' 10"Now, as you can see, the Lord has kept me alive and well as he promised for all these forty-five years since Moses made this promise—even while Israel wandered in the wilderness. Today I am eighty-five years old. 11I am as strong now as I was when Moses sent me on that journey, and I can still travel and fight as well as I could then. 12So give me the hill country that the Lord promised me. You will remember that as scouts we found the descendants of Anak living there in great, walled towns. But if the Lord is with me, I will drive them out of the land, just as the Lord said." 13So Joshua blessed Caleb son of Jephunneh and gave Hebron to him as his portion of land.*
>
> Joshua 14:9–13 (NLT)

I would have loved to have been in the company of those

men when Caleb addressed Joshua. I don't believe Joshua needed reminding of Caleb's heart. Caleb's commitment, attitude and deeds throughout every challenge were reminders not only to Joshua but to everyone. His was a kindred heart to Joshua's, and it carried the people of Israel fully into the purposes of God. It carried the men and their families; it influenced other nations both geographically and spiritually. It not only framed hope, but flagrantly displayed hope to encourage future generations.

> "Hope deferred makes the heart sick, but a dream fulfilled is a tree of life."
>
> Proverbs 13:12

Although the lives of Joshua and Caleb contained a promise, there were seasons where the promise was deferred. Yet within each of them was a commitment to trust in things both tangible and mysterious, coming together in heart and spirit—a quality described in the Bible as *wholehearted*.

Even though I think of myself as wholehearted, I sometimes struggle. I haven't arrived; it's a journey. But I believe that with God's grace, being wholehearted is possible. I'm not sure what that looks like in today's modern world of budgets and deadlines, commitments and bylines. But I know it's needed for our marriages, our families, our churches and communities. If we are to influence our workplace, the marketplace, our regions, states and nations, we have to be wholehearted. It is the only way we will reach the nations and influence them. I have a conviction in my spirit that God is still looking for men and women who will serve him fully--wholeheartedly. The earth needs people like Joshua and Caleb… now!

There are many things I've yet to learn about reaching that

place in heart, spirit and commitment. But there is one thing I do know with certainty. It starts with a decision and a declaration—the same decision and declaration that Caleb made in Joshua 14.

> *"But my brothers who went up with me made the hearts of the people melt with fear. I, however, followed the Lord my God wholeheartedly."*
>
> Joshua 14:8 (NIV)

This book has been a hope and longing of mine for a number of years. The Bible says that *"a longing fulfilled is as a tree of life"* (Proverbs 13:12). My hope is that by sharing some of my journey, testimonies and insights, you will be inspired to live differently. To some, it may be just a reminder of the call on your life. To others, it may be the challenge to step out of the ordinary and into the extraordinary things of God. Hopefully to all, it will lead to life of relationship with Jesus. Sometimes the reminder of what we have been rescued from, and released into, is necessary to continue in the living decision and declaration of being wholehearted.

I'm in.

How about you?

About The Author

Jeff Ecklund is the lead pastor of a great church in the Panhandle of North Idaho where he speaks weekly sharing Biblical principles, ministering to families and singles alike. He is a skilled communicator who is able to convey information as well as bring inspiration.

Jeff began his ministry career as a Christian musician and traveled for 8 years with a contemporary Christian music group in the Pacific Northwest. Jeff has authored and co-authored nearly 100 songs on 5 recording projects and has helped produce a number of other artist's projects. He is a gifted acoustic and electric guitar player.

Jeff began leading, speaking and writing in a pastoral ministry internship in his home church in Eastern Washington. He served as worship leader and youth pastor. He was ordained as an associate pastor in his home church and served for 17 years there until he and his wife were called to a church in central Idaho as lead pastors. The Ecklunds served in this church for 7 years. During these years they built up the church, merged two like-minded churches together and built a new church. They were called away from central Idaho to pastor in north Idaho, where they currently serve today. Jeff also serves as a support to other pastors, churches and leadership teams through counsel and leadership dynamics.

An avid outdoor sportsman, Jeff enjoys these activities whenever he can and welcomes any opportunity to participate in these activities to recreate and build relationships. Jeff's favorite outdoor sports are fishing, bow hunting, and bird hunting with his gun dogs by his side.

Jeff has been married to his wife Robie for 37 years. They met through a mutual friend and shared an interest in music, which lead them forward into the secular music profession. They made a decision following that to pursue music that expressed their Christian core values. The Ecklunds have two married sons, two daughters in law and 7 grandchildren.

It has been Jeff's dream for over 30 years to write a book. The book you are now holding is the realization of that dream.

Jeff can be reached at j.ecklund@hotmail.com.

Made in the USA
San Bernardino, CA
04 March 2018